The American History Series

S ERIES E DITORS
John Hope Franklin, *Duke University*
A. S. Eisenstadt, *Brooklyn College*

Any of books
Revin thesis explains his
thesis why it was good
and Relavts to class
3.5

Robert V. Remini
UNIVERSITY OF ILLINOIS AT CHICAGO

The Jacksonian Era

SECOND EDITION

HARLAN DAVIDSON, INC.
WHEELING, ILLINOIS 60090-6000

Library of Congress Cataloging-in-Publication Data

Remini, Robert Vincent, 1921–
    The Jacksonian era / Robert V. Remini. — 2nd ed.
        p.   cm. — (The American history series)
    Includes bibliographical references and index.
    ISBN 0-88295-931-X
    1. United States—Politics and government—1829–1837.
2. United States—History—1815–1861. 3. Jackson, Andrew, 1767–1845. I.
Title. II. Series: American history series (Wheeling, Ill.)

E381.R415   1997
973.5'6—dc20   96-41307

Cover illustration: Detail of drawing by Howard Pyle, "General Jackson,
President-Elect, on his way to Washington." *Courtesy Library of Congress*
613487 262-5412

Manufactured in the United States of America
04 03 02 3 4 5 TS

FOREWORD

Every generation writes its own history for the reason that it sees the past in the foreshortened perspective of its own experience. This has surely been true of the writing of American history. The practical aim of our historiography is to give us a more informed sense of where we are going by helping us understand the road we took in getting where we are. As the nature and dimensions of American life are changing, so too are the themes of our historical writing. Today's scholars are hard at work reconsidering every major aspect of the nation's past: its politics, diplomacy, economy, society, recreation, mores and values, as well as status, ethnic, race, sexual, and family relations. The lists of series titles that appear on the inside covers of this book will show at once that our historians are ever broadening the range of their studies.

The aim of this series is to offer our readers a survey of what today's historians are saying about the central themes and aspects of the American past. To do this, we have invited to write for the series only scholars who have made notable contributions to the respective fields in which they are working. Drawing on primary and secondary materials, each volume presents a factual and narrative account of its particular subject, one that affords readers a basis for perceiving its larger dimensions and importance. Conscious that readers respond to the closeness and immediacy of a subject, each of our authors seeks to restore the past as an actual present, to revive it as a living reality. The individuals and groups who figure in the pages of our books appear as real people who once were looking for survival and fulfillment. Aware that historical subjects are often matters of controversy, our authors present their own findings and conclusions. Each volume closes with an extensive critical essay on the writings of the major authorities on its particular theme.

The books in this series are primarily designed for use in both basic and advanced courses in American history, on the undergraduate and graduate levels. Such a series has a particular value these days, when the format of American history courses is being altered to accommodate a greater diversity of reading materials. The series offers a number of distinct advantages. It extends the dimensions of regular course work. It makes clear that the study of our past is, more than the student might otherwise understand, at once complex, profound, and absorbing. It presents that past as a subject of continuing interest and fresh investigation.

For these reasons the series strongly invites an interest that far exceeds the walls of academe. The work of experts in their respective fields, it puts at the disposal of all readers the rich findings of historical inquiry, an invitation to join, in major fields of research, those who are pondering anew the central themes and aspects of our past.

And, going beyond the confines of the classroom, it reminds the general reader no less than the university student that in each successive generation of the ever-changing American adventure, from its very start until our own day, men and women and children were facing their daily problems and attempting, as we are now, to live their lives and to make their way.

John Hope Franklin
A. S. Eisenstadt

CONTENTS

PREFACE TO THE SECOND EDITION

What is so wonderful about the Jacksonian era is the fact that after more than a hundred years it remains a controversial period in American history, and historians regularly provide us with new interpretations and new evaluations to explain what and why events occurred and individuals behaved as they did. And not surprisingly, Jackson himself remains a figure of dispute. His treatment of Native Americans, his War against the Bank of the United States, his handling of such questions as the tariff and internal improvements, and his response to the market revolution continue to invite reexamination by scholars.

In presenting this second edition I have tried to be responsive to the newer viewpoints that have been forthcoming since the book's initial publication, although I confess I have not always been in sympathy with some of the more recent findings. But there can be no question that current studies of the market revolution, the role of women, religious reforms and social developments have added immeasurably to our understanding of this era.

In addition, new documents keep coming to light which frequently provide fresh information and/or amplify certain aspects of the historical record. A good example is the discovery a few years ago of a document in the archives of Seville, Spain, that revealed that Jackson had taken an oath of loyalty to the King of Spain when he established business connections in Natchez in 1789. At that time the Natchez area as well as Louisiana and the

Floridas were under Spanish rule. This second edition provides both a discussion of the document and, in the picture section—which is another addition to this book—a copy of the last page of the document on which Jackson signed his name can be seen. Since writing this book almost ten years ago I have completed biographies of Henry Clay and Daniel Webster and I have included much more information about these two important statesman in this book. I have also rewritten extended sections on the religious reforms of the period and added important new titles to the bibliography.

For this second edition I wish to acknowledge the excellent assistance of Lucy Herz, production editor at Harlan Davidson Inc., and Andrew Davidson, editor and vice president of the company. I am grateful to them both.

Robert V. Remini

In memory of Harlan Davidson

Jackson Forever!

The Hero of Two Wars and of Orleans!

The Man of the People!

HE WHO COULD NOT BARTER NOR BARGAIN FOR THE

PRESIDENCY!

Who, although "A Military Chieftain," raised the purity of Elections and of the Electors, MORE than the Office of PRESIDENT itself! Although the greatest in the gift of his countrymen, and the highest in point of dignity of any in the world,

BECAUSE

It should be derived from the

PEOPLE!

No Gag laws! No Black Cockades! No Reign of Terror! No Standing Army or Navy Officers, when under the pay of Government, to browbeat, or

KNOCK DOWN

Old Revolutionary Characters, or our Representatives while in the discharge of their duty. To the Polls then, and vote for those who will support

OLD HICKORY

AND THE ELECTORAL LAW.

Courtesy of the New York Historical Society

CHAPTER ONE

A Hero for an Age

The American army crouched behind a shallow ditch that ran more than half a mile from the Mississippi River to a cypress swamp and had been fortified with a five-foot-high mud rampart. Several hundred yards in front of this rag-tag collection of American regulars, militiamen, and volunteers sprawled a magnificent British army, the conquerors of Napoleon, tensely awaiting the rocket flare that would signal the start of the Battle of New Orleans.

It was the 8th of January, 1815, and at dawn a mist rose from the Mississippi and slowly rolled across the plain separating the two armies. Within a short time it began drifting away. Suddenly, near the swamp, a Congreve rocket screeched into the sky, followed by a second rocket that ascended from a point next to the river. These two frightening incendiaries announced to the British soldiers that all was prepared and ready and that they were to proceed immediately to carry the American line by storm.

A company of redcoats from the center of the British line surged forward, displaying magnificent military discipline. Drums started beating a steady rhythm to accompany the advancing column. The Americans cheered as they watched their brightly colored targets moving toward them. Guns trained on these unwelcome invaders. Suddenly, the entire American line exploded in gunfire. Artillery, rifles, small arms poured their death into the faces of these hapless warriors as a band behind the rampart struck up "Yankee Doodle." The ranks of Americans rotated: first one line delivered its deadly fire and stepped back to reload while a second line took its place, fired, and then retreated. Still a third line delivered its destruction so that the fire remained constant. As the barrage of gunfire thundered from the mud rampart, volley after volley after volley, scores of redcoats crumpled to the ground.

Standing behind the American line, slightly left of center, General Andrew Jackson of Tennessee called encouragement to his men. This long, thin shaft of steely determination looked every inch the proud commander. He stood slightly more than six feet tall and he weighed no more than 145 lbs. His face was narrow, his features sharp, accentuated by a lantern jaw and clear blue eyes that seemed to strike sparks when a passion surged within him. He looked to the left, and then to the right. "Give it to them, my boys," he shouted. "Let us finish the business to-day."

"Fire! fire!" cried General William Carroll to the Tennessee and Kentucky riflemen, and these skilled frontiersmen picked off the scarlet-colored uniforms racing toward them with unbelievable accuracy. They decimated the column. One British officer claimed he had never seen a more destructive fire poured down upon a single line of men.

The flashing and roaring hell that greeted the charging redcoats finally brought them to a halt. The horror before them proved too great to withstand. The British army reeled, broke, and finally fled the field, leaving behind hundreds of dead and wounded, many piled on top of one another.

The commanding officer of the British army, Lieutenant General Sir Edward Michael Pakenham, was killed in the action. So, too, were all the other senior British officers in the forward position. Small wonder the rank and file lost heart and fled the carnage that lay strewn before the mud ditch. "The field was completely red," reported one newspaper shortly afterward, "covered with dead and wounded laying in heaps." General Jackson stared in shocked amazement at the ghastly scene. "I never had so grand and awful an idea of the resurrection as on that day," he wrote, as wounded bodies at the bottom of the heaps began to move and rise up. These men were still alive and struggling to free themselves from the lifeless bodies lying on top of them.

Over 2,000 British soldiers were killed, wounded, or declared missing in action; General Jackson reported 13 Americans killed, 39 wounded, and 19 missing in action. It was a stupendous victory, one never achieved before in the history of American arms. No battle of the Revolution even approached the magnitude of this triumph. And to think an unimposing collection of frontiersmen, volunteers, pirates, blacks, and some regular army men had pulverized the army that had defeated the great Napoleon. At first it was hard to believe. Too good to be true. But when the realization of what had been accomplished along a swampy plain outside of New Orleans finally sank in, the American people rapturously shouted their thanksgiving. They blessed Andrew Jackson and his men for restoring their faith in themselves, in their ability to fight for their country and in the republican principles on which it was founded. Now, at last, the rest of the world knew that the United States could defend itself and preserve its independence from the greatest powers on earth.

The Battle of New Orleans was the last important military engagement of the War of 1812. As a matter of fact it was fought shortly after a peace treaty had been signed between Great Britain and the United States in Ghent, Belgium, on Christmas Eve, 1814, but before news of the treaty had crossed the Atlantic Ocean. And because it was such a stupendous victory it boosted the nation's morale and self-confidence. The American people could now hold their heads up high. As John Quincy Adams, one of the U.S. ministers at Ghent who negotiated the treaty of peace, told the Secretary of State a little over a month before the Battle of New Orleans: "We shall have no valuable friends in Europe until we have proved that we can defend ourselves without them. There will be friends enough, if we can maintain our own cause by our own resources."

Now, at last, they had that victory. They had finally shown the rest of the world what they could do. Never again did the American people need to prove to themselves or anyone else that their freedom was legitimately won. It was a psychological boost of incalculable proportions and they credited it all to Andrew Jackson. They never forgot what he had done for the country in providing a total and devastating defeat of British arms on the field of battle. The American people never lost their sense of pride in his achievement. Many of them swore that they would remember the 8th of January like the 4th of July. Both dates, they believed, would be forever inscribed in the "minds and hearts of all true Americans." For both dates celebrated the nation's pledge to preserve freedom for all. Many Americans thereafter knew Jackson simply as the "Hero of New Orleans," although his soldiers had earlier given him the nickname "Old Hickory" out of their love and respect for his courage, strength, and indomitable will.

Because of this colossal victory the American people could deny Jackson nothing—including the presidency. As far as they were concerned it was impossible to repay him in any tangible way. The victory—indeed, the entire war—had given Americans what they essentially lacked, said one foreigner, "a national character founded on a glory common to all."

What made it all the more remarkable was the fact that Jackson had little military experience and had come from humble origins. He was born on March 15, 1767, in the Waxhaw settlement located along the northwestern frontier of South Carolina, an area of piney woods and soil of red clay. His father died before he was born and his mother succumbed to cholera while nursing captive American soldiers held aboard British prison ships in Charleston harbor during the Revolution. He himself was captured, slashed on the wrist and forehead by a British officer, and taken to a prison camp, where he contracted smallpox. Both his older brothers died during the Revolution but he survived after a long bout with the smallpox. Orphaned and pretty much left to his own devices, he traveled north to Salisbury, North Carolina, where he studied law in the law office of Spruce McCay. He led a wild, undisciplined life and gained a reputation as "the most roaring, rollicking, game-cocking, horse-racing, card-playing, mischievous fellow, that ever lived in Salisbury." Years later the good people of Salisbury heard that Jackson was running for the presidency. "What," cried one. "Jackson up for the President? Jackson? Andrew Jackson? The Jackson that used to live in Salisbury? Why, when he was here, he was such a rake that my husband would not bring him into the house! . . . Well, if Andrew Jackson can be President, anybody can!"

After his admission to the bar the twenty-one-year-old Jackson decided his best opportunities lay further west across the Alleghenies, and so he packed his gun, several letters of introduction, and a few belongings, and rode out to Nashville, Tennessee. Along the way he got into a quarrel with another lawyer and challenged him to a duel. The two men met just a little after sundown to settle their dispute with guns. Fortunately, both missed, and Jackson walked away from his first duel unscathed. He arrived in Nashville on October 26, 1788. Sensitive to a fault about his honor, ambitious, a man who liked to take charge, courteous but hotheaded and quick to anger, Jackson established himself as a lawyer and began an extensive trading business opening a store and extending his trading operation as far south as Natchez, Mississippi. At the time Natchez was claimed by Spain and anyone wishing to settle or conduct business in the town was required by law to take an oath of loyalty to the King of Spain. Without a moment's hesitation Jackson obeyed. On July 15, 1789, he stood before the Spanish governor, placed his hand on the Bible and swore that he would not "conspire against the Spanish nation" but "would defend it and help it" with all his "might, will and power," subjecting himself to "all Spanish Laws . . . orders, proclamations, and edicts of the Kingdom." With this oath of allegiance Andrew Jackson became a vassal of the King of Spain. But he was a pragmatic realist. Expediency often played an important role in his actions throughout his life. To operate his trading business in Natchez within the law he had to take the oath. Undoubtedly he took it without giving it a second thought. Like hundreds of other Americans before and after him, he did what necessity dictated. He also married Rachel Donelson in Natchez. She came from one of the first families of Tennessee. She was already married to Lewis Robards when Jackson first met her in Nashville. She was a lively girl, full of bounce and energy, but the roaring, rollicking, red-haired Jackson was more than a match for her. Robards, on the other hand, was neurotically suspicious of his wife and constantly quarreled with her about her behavior. They divorced—or so everyone thought—and she ran off with Jackson to Natchez to be married. Later she discovered that the divorce had not yet been granted. Technically she was a bigamist, and the couple lived together for two years. Finally, on January 17, 1794, when the divorce was finally granted, Rachel "remarried" Jackson. It can be imagined how many divorced women could be found in the United States in 1794, let alone in Tennessee, let alone the wife of a future President. It also says something important about Andrew Jackson that he married a divorced woman, that he was willing to risk possible ostracism by society for his action. It says something important about the love he bore Rachel. An extraordinary relationship existed between them, and it grew ever stronger over the years.

Despite the shaky beginning to his marital life, Jackson prospered as a lawyer, trader, and planter. He was elected to the convention that wrote Tennessee's constitution, and he was sent to Congress as the state's first and only member of the House of Representatives. In 1797 he was elected to the U.S. Senate but the office did not suit his taste, and he resigned after a short term and accepted appointment as a judge of the Superior Court of Tennessee. As a judge it was said that his opinions were "short, untechnical, unlearned, sometimes ungrammatical, and generally right."

Also, by election, he won command of the Tennessee militia in 1802 with the rank of Major General. He had campaigned for several years to win this office because it could (as it subsequently did) bring him the fame he so desperately wanted to achieve. His first opportunity for glory came in 1813 when the Creek Indians rose against white settlers in Alabama and he was summoned by the governor to lead his troops to quell the uprising. After a series of engagements and indescribable hardships, General Jackson defeated the Creeks at the Battle of Horseshoe Bend on March 27, 1814. He imposed a draconian peace treaty on the Indians and then marched his men to New Orleans where he repelled the British invasion and won recognition as the "saviour of his country."

A few years after the War of 1812, President James Monroe ordered him against the Seminole nation in Spanish-held Florida, who had been initiating raids along the American frontier. But the order was purposely vague and gave him wide latitude in coping with both the Indians and Spanish. Nevertheless he wrote the President and asked for formal permission to seize Florida, despite his earlier oath of allegiance to Spain. Under the impression that permission had been granted, Jackson promptly invaded, executed two English subjects for inciting and arming the Indians, and seized Florida from the Spanish. The province was ultimately ceded to the United States for $5 million in claims owed by Spain to American citizens. According to the terms of the Adams-Onís Treaty, or the Transcontinental Treaty, as it is sometimes called, signed in 1819, Spain not only relinquished Florida, but also surrendered its claims to the Oregon country, thereby transforming the United States into a transcontinental power. The future greatness of the nation was virtually assured by this single stroke.

Not much later, when Jackson began showing signs of interest in running for the presidency, a few traditionalists expressed skepticism. They were fully prepared to acknowledge Jackson's great military contribution to the Republic, but they did not believe that that distinction qualified him for the presidency. He may have been expert in annihilating Indians, Spaniards, and Britons, but he clearly did not have the experience, education, temperament, and intelligence essential in a chief executive. Surely the presidential office required more than military skill and popularity among the electorate. Surely it demanded statesmanship and an outstanding record of unselfish service on behalf of the public good. But the American people shrugged their indifference to this argument. As far as they were concerned, they loved, respected, admired, and trusted Andrew Jackson, and that was good enough reason in their minds to seat him in the White House as successor to the great men of the Revolutionary generation.

Jackson was not alone in having to convince some Americans that he was worthy of elective office despite his threadbare record as a public servant. Compared to such previous Presidents as George Washington, John Adams, Thomas Jefferson, James Madison, and James Monroe—the first five Presidents—he could not begin to match their record of accomplishments. But who could? The revolutionary generation had produced an extraordinary crop of statesmen. They wrote and signed the Declaration, Articles of Confederation, the Constitution, and, in many instances, the constitutions of their individual states. But most of these heroes were now gone, having either died or retired. And who could ever compare to them? Who of the succeeding generation could stand before the American people and invite their support when they had accomplished relatively little of note, when they could offer nothing substantial to inspire the electorate's confidence in their ability to rule the nation and protect individual freedom?

Yet they were not a hapless generation. There were several statesmen of extraordinary stature and ability among them. Men like John Quincy Adams, son of the second President and a distinguished diplomat; Henry Clay of Kentucky, Speaker of the House of Representatives, who with Adams and three others had participated in the negotiations that produced the peace treaty ending the War of 1812; John C. Calhoun of South Carolina, a brilliant logician and political scientist and a superb Secretary of War during Monroe's administration; Daniel Webster of Massachusetts, a powerful orator and exponent of American capitalism whose majestic voice in debate never failed to thrill his listeners; and Martin Van Buren of New York, the archetypical politician of the new age that emerged after the War of 1812.

All of these men, at one time or another, seriously aspired to the presidency. In no conceivable way could they compare their personal careers with those of the Founding Fathers. Nor did they try. True, Jackson had New Orleans—and that, as it turned out, proved more than sufficient for his lifetime. It was even said that Americans voted for him fifteen years after his death. But for other presidential aspirants there was a real problem. None of them had ever fought for their country; and none had signed the Declaration, nor participated in writing or ratifying the Constitution. Without such imposing credentials they were forced to substitute something else in order to inspire credence in the legitimacy of their right to lead and direct the affairs of the nation. Ultimately, what they found and used to advance their political careers was the party system, even though the Founding Fathers frowned on parties and tended to regard them as factions of ambitious men banded together to achieve their own selfish ends. George Washington and John Adams had been particularly vociferous in their denunciation of parties. They regarded parties as pernicious, a threat to republicanism, and promoters of corruption. Said John Adams: The "division of the republic into two great parties . . . is to be dreaded as the greatest political evil under our Constitution."

Despite the fears and denunciations of many of the Founders of the nation, a two-party system did in fact develop during the administration of President George Washington. The Republican party emerged behind the leadership of the Secretary of State, Thomas Jefferson, and his friend and colleague in the House of Representatives, James Madison. These men and others felt compelled to organize themselves to challenge the policies of the Secretary of the Treasury, Alexander Hamilton, who led a faction supporting the administration that called itself the Federalist party. The Federalists, who sought to centralize authority and award the national government increased powers, were successful in controlling the government until 1800, when John Adams lost his bid for reelection to the presidency and Thomas Jefferson was selected in his stead. During the War of 1812 some Federalists from New England expressed their anger and concern with the central government by meeting in convention at Hartford, Connecticut, and proposing a number of amendments to the Constitution that would address their grievances. Since the Hartford Convention was a secret enclave, many Americans suspected it of fomenting treason. The victory at New Orleans and the conclusion of a peace treaty ending the War of 1812 discredited both the Hartford Convention and the Federalist party. Although the party continued to play a somewhat active role in state politics, it went into an immediate decline on the national level and no longer offered candidates in presidential elections.

That left the Republican party as the single party running the country. Men of opposing ideological positions crowded into it, and one newspaper presumed to characterize the period following the War of 1812 as an "Era of Good Feelings." But political feelings around the country were just as intense and bitter over issues as they had been when two national parties vied with each other for control of the central government.

Because the two parties had run the country effectively for over twenty years, the old complaints about them, especially the claim that they were little more than enclaves of squabbling, greedy, and ambitious men, slowly dissipated. By the time war broke out against Great Britain in 1812, a great many Americans had come to regard the party structure as healthy and useful.

With the appearance of men like Van Buren, Clay, Calhoun, Webster, and others of this second generation of American statesmen there was a further move away from the fears about parties. There was a new sense of the value and purpose of such organizations. A man like Van Buren, who appreciated that his career depended on the support a party could provide for his candidacy to office, actually came to believe that parties were essential to the proper operation of the Republic. Parties were not merely useful or valuable but rather the *sine qua non* for the orderly and stable running of the government. The only way to preserve a democracy, he preached, was to have two organized parties holding different principles and openly arrayed against each other. The natural tensions within society could then find release in the regular contest between these opposing groups. In the normal course of events the people would side with one party for a period of time and when they grew tired of that party or were offended by its actions they would dismiss it and turn to the opposing party for a change of men and measures. Such a regular shifting of political forces back and forth between parties would check misuse of power and safeguard the liberty of all. As Van Buren saw it, the Era of Good Feelings was an anomaly—worse, a lively threat that one party could become complacent and indifferent to the will and needs of its constituents. It would soon become corrupt and jeopardize the life and safety of the Republic.

And because the American people were and remain essentially conservative in their political thinking, demanding stability and the protection of life and property, a two-party system was the only way to guarantee that stability. A multi-party system can and often does necessitate coalitions among the several parties in order to form a government. But these coalitions frequently unravel and bring down the government, forcing new elections.

To Van Buren and the horde of professional politicians who appeared with him after the War of 1812, two parties, not one or more, was the only way the United States could survive as a republic of free men and women. Moreover, to them a party was not simply a cadre of men blindly obeying the dictates of their leaders and never questioning the policies and purposes of the party. Even though Van Buren exulted party discipline and all the instruments by which it could be instilled into the faithful, nevertheless he appreciated the true purpose of a two-party system in a democratic society. He was an ideologue, as were most political leaders at the beginning of the nineteenth century. He believed that parties must stand for certain principles, opposing others, and that they must practice certain republican values. Otherwise, the public soon grows tired of them and they sink, like the Federalist party, into oblivion.

Martin Van Buren, born on December 5, 1782, in the tiny village of Kinderhook, Columbia County, New York, was the first President actually born in the United States. Son of a tavern keeper, he received his first and possibly his most valuable education in learning to deal with people while helping his father run the establishment. After a formal education at the village academy he studied law and began his practice in 1803. He joined the Republican party, rose rapidly through the ranks, first as surrogate of Columbia County, and then as senator in the upper house of the New York state legislature. Within ten years of his arrival in Albany, the state capital, he gained control of the Republican party mainly because of his genius for political organization. When he was elected to the United States Senate in 1821 he created the Albany Regency, a group of skillful and powerful party leaders, to run the state in his absence.

In Washington Van Buren assumed leadership of the most conservative wing of the Republican party, called Radicals by some. His success as a party leader—apart from his organizing skills—stemmed in large measure from his personal charm and ingratiating manner. A short man, with light sandy hair and a prominent forehead, he was courteous to all and possessed the "high art of blending dignity with ease and suavity." He was, said one man, "as polished and captivating a person in the social circle as America has ever known. . . ." Because his political skills seemed at times to verge on the miraculous, a lot of people began to call him "the Little Magician."

Van Buren claimed to follow the republican doctrines of Thomas Jefferson. That meant he opposed a strong central government and a loose interpretation of the Constitution. That also meant he regarded the states as wholesome counterweights to the national government and that the rights of the states must be defended by all who concerned themselves with preserving liberty. Van Buren opposed the idea of the federal government sponsoring public works. The fact that his state of New York had undertaken the building of the Erie Canal no doubt strengthened his prejudices against internal improvements from Washington. But he genuinely opposed federally sponsored public works on principle, arguing that it dangerously inflated the power of the central government at the expense of the states. Finally, he advocated economy in operating the government.

Both Van Buren and Jackson espoused this republican philosophy, a philosophy that Jackson called these "good old jeffersonian

Democratic republican principles." They were conservative principles, but to Jackson they provided the essential foundation of free government and a free society. And because Van Buren cared deeply about republicanism he worried over the effects of a sustained "Era of Good Feelings." A one-party system, in his mind, was destructive of honest and efficient government. A single party could place anyone in office, irrespective of their allegiance to sound principle; and loyalty to party could become the sole condition for office holding. A dictatorship of sorts could emerge. All of which to Van Buren guaranteed corruption and misconduct in office. Instead, he argued the benefits of the two-party system, and in the winter of 1826–27 he took the first in a series of steps that ultimately resulted in the restoration of a viable two-party system.

This first step occurred during the administration of President John Quincy Adams. A combination of events set the process in motion. First, the election of Adams generated a storm of protest. In the presidential contest of 1824 he lost out in both the popular vote and the electoral vote to Andrew Jackson. But Jackson failed to win a majority of electors and so the election went to the House of Representatives for final determination as dictated by the Twelfth Amendment to the Constitution. There Henry Clay, in total disregard of the electoral results as well as explicit instructions from the Kentucky legislature, decided to use his considerable influence in the House to make Adams the sixth President of the United States.

Henry Clay was born on April 12, 1777, in Hanover County, Virginia, read law with Chancellor George Wythe and after obtaining his license moved to Lexington, Kentucky, at the age of twenty. He was immediately recognized as a superb lawyer and speaker. After a stint in the state's general assembly he subsequently won election to the U.S. Senate and later to the U.S. House of Representatives where he was chosen Speaker on the first ballot of the first day of the Congressional session. "Harry of the West," as his friends called him, transformed the office of Speaker by controlling membership of committees and determining which legislation would be brought to the entire House. Under his direction the Speaker became the second most powerful officer of the government after the President. Popular with his colleagues and repeatedly reelected, he served longer than any succeeding Speaker in the nineteenth century. As leader of the War Hawks he helped push President Madison into a declaration of war against Great Britain. He served with John Quincy Adams and others on the peace commission that ended the war in 1814, and then he returned to Congress. A fascinating man—hail-fellow, swaggering, impudent—Clay had a lively sense of humor and reputedly drank Bourbon in "heaping quantities." He was tall, almost cadaverous, with large hollows gouged in both cheeks and a thin line marking the location of his bloodless lips. As a public speaker he was supreme, often combining erudition with biting humor. One garrulous old Congressman gave a speech in the House and went on hour after hour, claiming to speak for future generations. "Yes," Clay interrupted, "and you seem determined to keep on talking until your audience arrives."

Clay lusted for the presidency—no other verb is as appropriate—and tried five times throughout his long career to win it. His first attempt and first failure came in 1824 when he was eliminated from the House election because he had the fewest electoral votes. As "king-maker," he threw his support to Adams who rewarded him with the position of secretary of state. The friends of Jackson accused the two men of having contracted a "corrupt bargain" to steal the presidency and deny the American people the right to choose their chief executive. "The will of the people has been thwarted," thundered Andrew Jackson.

Following this scandal, President Adams committed a grave blunder. In his first State of the Union address to Congress, he described a national program of public works which he, Clay, and other nationalistic-minded Republicans sincerely believed would benefit all Americans in every section of the country. He called for a vigorous program of internal improvements by the national government which even included the establishment of a national university and an astronomical observatory, creation of a naval academy similar to West Point, the exploration of the western territories and the northeastern coastline, and the building of an extensive system of roads, canals, and harbor installations. His brand of republicanism followed closely along lines first laid out by Clay. It was termed the "American System," and Clay argued in favor of federally sponsored internal improvements, a protective tariff to promote industry, and a national bank that would control and regulate the nation's credit and currency. Clay, Adams, and their followers—dubbed National Republicans at first but later called Whigs—felt the central government should be responsible for the nation's material and cultural well-being. So their national program necessarily strengthened the central government and required a loose interpretation of the Constitution in order to allow Congress the necessary powers to carry out such an ambitious program; and it meant expanding the amounts of money appropriated by Congress. Adams' blunder came when, in urging the passage of internal improvements, he admonished Congress not to give the rest of the world the impression that "we are palsied by the will of our constituents." It was an unfortunate expression which seemed to prove that Adams had no regard at all for popular opinion.

Although the National Republicans could not field a candidate with the popularity of an Andrew Jackson, they did have leaders of uncommon talent and commitment to public service, including, besides Clay, John Quincy Adams and Daniel Webster. If Clay was popular, friendly and outgoing, Adams was another breed altogether. Dour, almost forbidding at times, critical of everyone including himself, and perpetually selfrighteous, he himself admitted that he was "a man of reserved, cold, austere and forbidding manners." Born in 1767 (the same year as Jackson) in Braintree, Massachusetts, the eldest son of John and Abigail Adams, he was groomed by his parents for high office, and he did not fail them. A successful diplomat who, at different times, headed the American missions to the Netherlands, Portugal, Prussia, and Russia, as well as a commissioner who helped prepare the Treaty of Ghent, Adams became secretary of state under President Monroe, and in the House election of 1825 was himself chosen President of the United States.

In their many battles with the Jacksonians, Clay and Adams had the considerable assistance of Daniel Webster, the godlike Daniel, as he was sometimes called on account of his extraordinary oratorical powers. Born in New Hampshire in 1782 (the same year as Van Buren and Calhoun), he went to Dartmouth College, won election to Congress, and later moved to Boston because he believed that Massachusetts held many more opportunities for an ambitious and talented lawyer and politician. He was soon arguing cases before the U.S. Supreme Court and in 1823 was elected to Congress, first as a Representative and later as Senator. During the years following the War of 1812, as New England's attraction to Henry Clay's American System became more pronounced, Webster's approval of the system also mounted. Soon he was advocating strong government involvement in the economic well-being of the country, including the heroic program delivered in President Adams's State of the Union message to Congress for lighthouses, roads, canals, and a university. Swarthy, with bushy eyebrows and jet black hair and eyes, he was also known as Black Dan. He had a hypnotic stare that could freeze a victim in his tracks. One minister remembered looking down from the pulpit and seeing Webster gazing intently at him. Black Dan, he said, fixed "such great, staring black eyes upon me that I was frightened out of my wits."

In many respects Adams's program was a breathtaking vision of what the country could do for itself. But Jackson, Van Buren, and their many friends were appalled. They foresaw disaster. They predicted an early end to the Republic if such expenditures were approved. They declared the program blatantly unconstitutional and a mockery of the republican principles on which the country had been founded. They ridiculed Adams's nationalistic program of improvement as a preposterous attempt "to build light-houses in the sky." As a result of his deep concern over the direction Adams and Clay wished to take the nation, Van Buren approached Vice President John C. Calhoun in the winter of 1826–27 and suggested the need to unite their forces against the administration.

Calhoun had set his sights on the presidency during the years he served as Secretary of War under President Monroe, but when he found his supporters deserting to Jackson in 1823 he decided to accept instead a bid for the vice presidential office and bide his time. He won the office with virtually no opposition. Born in South Carolina on March 18, 1782, he graduated from Yale, studied law at Tapping Reeve's school at Litchfield, Connecticut, and was later elected to the House of Representatives, where he became a War Hawk. He frequently looked cold and forbidding, as though pondering some "metaphysical abstraction." Harriet Martineau, the English visitor, said he looked as though he had never been born and could never be extinguished. She called him the "cast iron man." His voice was sharp and somewhat reedy. When he spoke in Congress his words came quickly in near-staccato fashion but always with such precise enunciation that every word was distinctly heard. He was asked by President Monroe in 1817 to join his cabinet as Secretary of War and succeeded in reorganizing and revitalizing that department. A man of powerful intellect and ambition, handsome, with dark, flashing eyes, he now used his position as Vice President to annoy and harass the Adams administration.

When Calhoun met Van Buren to discuss the political future and what they should do about it, he was very wary of "the Little Magician," knowing his reputation. But he listened carefully to what the *New Yorker* had to say and he soon found that he liked what he heard. We must, Van Buren said, "draw anew the old Party lines." We must substitute *"party principle'* for *personal preference."* "In all the states," he went on, "the division between Republicans and Federalists is still kept up and cannot be laid aside.... We must always have party distinctions and the old ones are the best of which the nature of the case admits. Political combinations between the inhabitants of the different states are unavoidable and the most natural and beneficial to the country is that between the planters of the South and the plain Republicans of the North. The country has once flourished under a party thus constituted and may again."

In uniting the plain Republicans of the North with the planters of the South, Van Buren proposed that they back Andrew Jackson for the presidency. In Jackson the party had a man who was universally loved and certain to carry the election. But, continued Van Buren, "his election, as the result of his military services without reference to party . . . would be one thing. His election as the result of a combined and concerted effort of a political party, holding in the main, to certain tenets and opposed to certain prevailing principles, might be another and a far different thing."

Most appropriately, Van Buren planned to structure a national organization behind Jackson in order to insure his ultimate victory and prevent a recurrence of the last election. Of course such an organization, after it had emerged, did not have all the characteristics found in modern political parties. But it did include a national newspaper located in Washington to speak authoritatively to the party faithful. In time the propaganda apparatus was said to include "a chain of newspaper posts, from the New England States to Louisiana, and branching off through Lexington to the Western States." The friends of the Adams administration later accused Van Buren of attempting to regulate "the popular election by means of organized clubs in the States, and organized presses everywhere."

Calhoun agreed with Van Buren's arguments about the necessity of uniting their respective factions and he therefore joined him in support of Jackson's election in 1828. Their initial alliance later grew into an organization that called itself the Democratic party. This party took particular delight in celebrating the candidacy of General Andrew Jackson. It found that Old Hickory's personality and accomplishments enhanced their ability to present him as an attractive and viable candidate. Indeed his career and personality stirred the imagination of Democratic leaders around the country. They devised new methods or improved old ones to get across the message that Andrew Jackson was the "man of the people" who saved the nation from invasion and possible defeat and domination by Great Britain and thereby showed the world that Americans could protect and preserve their liberty. Since Jackson had become a symbol of the best in American life, the party leaders adopted the obvious symbol of the hickory leaf to rouse the masses and get them to shout their support for "Old Hickory." Hickory brooms, hickory canes, hickory sticks appeared everywhere—on steeples, poles, on steamboats, stage coaches, at crossroads, and in the hands of all who would wave them to salute the "Old Hero of New Orleans." "In every village, as well as upon the corners of many city streets," hickory poles were erected. "Many of these poles were standing as late as 1845," recorded one contemporary, "rotten momentoes [sic] of the delirium of 1828." The National Republicans were outraged by this debasement of the political process. "Planting hickory trees!" snorted the Washington National Journal on May 24, 1828. "Odds nuts and drumsticks! What have hickory trees to do with republicanism and the great contest?"

The Democrats devised other gimmicks and devices to generate excitement for their ticket. "Jackson meetings" were held in every county where a Democratic organization existed, and to these meetings the mass electorate was invited to hear speeches extolling the virtues of the Old Hero. The masses were encouraged to shout their approval for a presidential candidate who could genuinely be labeled a true representative of all the people. "If we go into one of these meetings," declared an opposition newspaper, "of whom do we find them composed? Do we see there the solid, substantial, moral and reflecting yeomanry of the country? No. . . . They comprise a large portion of the dissolute, the noisy, the discontented, and designing of society." The Democratic press retorted with the claim that these so-called dissolute, noisy, and discontented were actually the "bone and muscle of American society. They are the People. The real People who understand that Gen. Jackson is one of them and will defend their interests and rights."

The Jacksonians were also very fond of parades and barbecues—anything to gather a listening audience, an audience that would appreciate the festivities and join in the celebration. In Baltimore a "Grand Barbecue" was scheduled to commemorate the successful defense of the when the British attacked during the War of 1812. But the Democrats expropriated the occasion and converted it into a Jackson rally. "I am told by a gentleman who is employed to erect the fixtures," Jackson was advised, "that three Bullocks are to be roasted, and each man is to wear a Hickory Leaf in his hat by way of designation." The celebration began with the firing of a cannon, followed by lengthy speeches about General Jackson's victories against the British and Indians, after which the crowd quaffed "their bumpers to his health." Before the barbecued beef was served the entire congregation sang a new song entitled "Hickory Wood."

Perhaps most spectacular of all were the parades the Democrats organized which wound their way down the main streets of cities and towns and came complete with fifes and drums, flags, floats, and transparencies. One such parade started with dozens of Democrats marching to the beat of a fife and drum corps and wearing no other insignia save "a twig of the sacred tree (hickory) in their hats." Trailing these faithful Jacksonians came "gigantic hickory poles," still live and crowned with green foliage, being carted in "on eight wheels for the purpose of being planted by the democracy on the eve of the election." These poles were drawn by eight horses, all decorated with "ribbons and mottoes."

The election of 1828 set a new low mark for vulgarity, gimmickry, and nonsensical hijinks. During the course of the campaign the questionable circumstances of Jackson's marriage were paraded before the public and no doubt contributed to Rachel's subsequent collapse and death. Jackson's mother was labeled "a COMMON PROSTITUTE" who was "brought to this country by the British soldiers! She afterwards married a MULATTO MAN, with whom she had several children, of which number General JACKSON IS ONE!!!" At the same time John Quincy Adams was labeled a pimp and accused of procuring for the Czar of Russia when serving as minister to that country. Jackson's military career was also attacked with the release of a handbill entitled "Some Account of the Bloody Deeds of GENERAL JACKSON" which showed a series of coffins and recounted the execution of six militia men charged with desertion during the Creek War. This "Coffin Hand Bill" as it was called prompted the Democrats into issuing a handbill of their own. It depicted a single coffin which read "SACRED to the Memory of SIR E. PACKENHAM and 2500 officers and soldiers ... cruelly shot to death by ANDREW JACKSON."

The campaign was one long disgraceful performance and showed how low politicians could sink to win votes. But it should be remembered that presidential candidates themselves did not campaign personally in those days and it was sometimes impossible for them to control what was said and written by their supporters.

When the contest finally ended Jackson had polled 647,276 popular votes to 508,064 for Adams. In the electoral college Jackson took 178 and Adams won 83. Jackson's sweep included practically everything south of the Potomac River and west of New Jersey. Adams carried New England, Delaware. New Jersey, and most of Maryland. Both candidates shared New York, with Jackson taking the larger portion.

Shortly after Jackson was notified of his victory, Rachel Jackson died of a heart attack and was buried in the garden of the Hermitage grounds where they lived. It was many weeks before the President-elect could stir himself to leave for Washington to take the oath of office. "My heart is nearly broke," he wrote. He blamed Rachel's death on "poltroons" who had repeated the slander about his marriage. And he faulted both Adams and Clay for not putting a stop to it. Indeed, he believed that Clay may have secretly provided information and direction to some of the worse publicists. Henry Clay, he wrote, "is the bases[t], meanest, scoundrel, that ever disgraced the image of his god—nothing too mean or low for him to condescend to, secretely to carry his cowardly and base purpose of slander into effect; even the aged and virtuous female, is not free from his secrete combination of base slander." While many called Clay "Harry of the West," Andrew Jackson called him "The *Judas* of the West."

The inauguration of General Andrew Jackson as the seventh President of the United States on March 4, 1829, provided one of the most colorful, glamorous, and exciting events in American history. It was a milestone in the political evolution of this country. It was called the First People's Inaugural, and it surely deserved that designation in more ways than one. Those who attended never forgot it. Thousands of people converged on the capital, "like the inundation of the northern barbarians into Rome," said one. "I never saw such a crowd here before," commented Daniel Webster. "Persons have come five hundred miles to see General Jackson, *and they really seem to think that the country is rescued from some dreadful danger!"*

The morning of the inauguration was balmy and mild, almost springlike. Early on, mobs began forming in the streets leading to the Capitol, where the outdoor ceremony would be held. According to one estimation, some 15–20,000 people appeared and crowded into every space available in front of the south portico. There was a great, agitated sea of humanity, in constant motion, pushing, shoving, jumping up and down.

Then all of a sudden the crowd spotted him coming through the portals of the Capitol. "Never can I forget the spectacle which presented itself on every side, nor the electrifying moment when the eager, expectant eyes of that vast and motley multitude caught sight of the tall and imposing form of their adored leader."

"Huzza! Huzza! Huzza!" they screamed. And General Andrew Jackson bowed low before the majesty of the people. Suddenly, as if by magic, the scene changed. "All hats were off at once, and the dark tint which usually pervades a mixed map of men was turned . . . into the bright hue of ten thousand upturned and exultant human faces, radiant with sudden joy."

After bowing to the "majesty of the people," Jackson seated himself between the two central columns of the Portico. Vice President John C. Calhoun sat on his left, and Chief Justice John Marshall on his right. When the screaming and cheering abated, Jackson rose and delivered his inaugural address. It was mercifully short. Among a number of things, he said he would protect the states in all of their rights, "taking care not to confound the powers they have reserved to themselves with those they have granted to the Confederacy." He expressed an ardent wish to extinguish the national debt but he would approve only those internal improvements that were authorized by the Constitution. He also said he favored a "judicious tariff." Finally, he declared that the electorate had recently shown in a number of ways that they wished their President to undertake "the task of *reform*, which will require particularly the correction of those abuses that have brought the patronage of the Federal Government into conflict with the freedom of elections, and . . . have placed or continued power in unfaithful or incompetent hands."

When he finished his address the Chief Justice administered the oath of office. The President then kissed the Bible, shook hands with John Marshall and again acknowledged the deafening roar of the crowd by bowing low before the assembled masses. To avoid the mob he exited through the Capitol, walked down the hill, and mounted a horse to ride to the White House.

Inside the mansion preparations had begun to allow the new President to meet visitors informally. But what turned up was never expected. A mob of farmers, gentlemen, boys, women, "rag-a-muffins," streamed through the White House. From the "highest and most polished, down to the most vulgar and gross in the nation," reported Associate Justice Joseph Story, put in an appearance. "The reign of KING MOB seemed triumphant," he added. Mrs. Samuel H. Smith, wife of the Maryland Senator, agreed. "The *Majesty of the People* had disappeared," she said. "The President, after having been *literally* nearly pressed to death & almost suffocated & torn to pieces by the people in their eagerness to shake hands with Old Hickory, had retreated through the back way or south front & had escaped to his lodgings at Gadsby's." It became such a riotous scene that barrels of punch were carried outside to the garden in order to draw the crowd from the house. The strategy worked, but some of the people jumped out of the windows to get at the refreshments. "We had a regular Saturnalia," laughed one Congressman. The mob constituted "one uninterrupted stream of mud and filth." Cut glass and china were broken in the melee. Men with "boots heavy with mud" stood on the "damask satin-covered chairs" to get a better look at the wild shenanigans. Still, with all the mayhem and destruction that took place, with all the animal American spirits at their most boisterous and vulgar, the arrival of General Andrew Jackson to power marked the beginning of a new era of the young republic. The sounds, smells, and sights of democracy were stirring around the country and they all seemed magnified in the inauguration of the seventh President. "It was a proud day for the people"—this

March 4, 1829—declared the *Argus of Western America.* "General Jackson is *their own* President . . . [and] he was greeted by them with an enthusiasm which bespoke him the Hero of a popular triumph."

CHAPTER TWO

Jacksonian Democracy

One of the things that made Jackson unique and contributed so vitally to the style and tone of this new political age was his absolute commitment to the idea of democracy. And by democracy he did not mean a system that could intrude upon, alter, or discount the popular will by substituting something or someone else in the name of better government, such as the House of Representatives had done in 1825 when they handed the presidency over to John Quincy Adams. A system that included a College of Electors, for example, wherein a small group of men could alter the results of a presidential election if they chose, was not democratic in Jackson's mind—say whatever else you may about it—and so he wanted to get rid of the College of Electors and repeatedly asked Congress, starting with his first annual message in December 1829, to initiate the process of amending the Constitution. Put simply, Jackson could not abide any "intermediary" agencies standing between the people and their government.

By democracy, Jackson meant majoritarian rule—pure and simple. "The people are the government," he said, "administering it by their agents; they are the Government, the sovereign power." In his first message to Congress he announced his creed: *"The majority is to govern,"* he declared; and he repeated this commitment at every opportunity. He felt that the electorate ought to select all its officials in Washington, starting with the President. He advocated a single term of either four or six years for the chief executive and he proposed this change to Congress. He also felt that Senators should be elected to four-year terms by the people, not by the state legislatures, which was the method until the 17th amendment, adopted in 1913, altered the process. Jackson would even have the electorate select its federal judges for terms of seven years, which indicated to some extent his total commitment to rotation of office as a means of democratizing the government.

Again, in his first message to Congress, President Jackson proposed a policy of *"reform"* by suggesting the need to "rotate" governmental offices on a regular basis. Office is considered a kind of property by some, he said, instead of acknowledging its true purpose, which is to be an instrument to serve the people. And most governmental offices, he continued, are "so plain and simple" that all men of intelligence may qualify. No one person has any more intrinsic right to hold office than any other. Thus, no one is wronged by removal after a period of, say, four years. Unless of course the person is corrupt or incompetent. Then that person should be removed immediately, no matter the length of tenure. "I can not but believe that more is lost by the long continuance of men in office than is generally to be gained by their experience. I submit, therefore, to your consideration whether the efficiency of the Government would not be promoted and official industry and integrity better secured by a general extension of the law which limits appointments to four years."

Jackson's argument for the principle of "rotation of office" was the argument of democracy. Offices exist to serve the people. No one has a special claim to office. There are no elites. No special class. Removal from office, therefore, is not intrinsically wrong. So when the people elect a new President it is only right that he be given the opportunity to bring into government the sort of people he needs to help him accomplish the tasks he was elected to perform. He ought not to be saddled with the holdouts of a previous administration who would most likely be indifferent, if not hostile, to the programs of the new President. Democracy requires that the decision of the people in the selection of their new chief executive should be reflected down to the last office holder—or so Jackson contended. And if his policy were implemented, he declared, then the notion of office as a specie of property would be terminated.

Although Jackson made a great noise about his policy of removal he actually dismissed relatively few men from government service. It has been shown that during his entire eight years as President he replaced no more than 10 percent of all office holders. In the first eighteen months of his presidency only 919 out of 10,093 employees were removed. When these figures are evaluated in terms of normal replacements due to death and resignation, plus those dismissed for misbehavior or incompetence, they constitute a very modest record of removal. Also, it has been pointed out that Jackson's appointees, in terms of their educational, social, and economic backgrounds, were hardly different from those of his predecessors in the presidential office. Government service was not really opened to the general public, as Jackson seemed to be demanding, but rather remained with the same class of bureaucrat that had always controlled the service. But what needs to be remembered is Jackson's commitment to the *principle* of rotation by which the democratic process could be advanced. Also, in all the changes he initiated while in office and all the changes he attempted to initiate, it should be kept in mind that what he did remained deeply rooted in tradition. In other words, Jackson's sense of the past and its value should not be underestimated. Historical continuity is never easily broken, and Jackson was more respectful of it than is generally appreciated. He can best be described, therefore, as both a "harbinger of change" and a great respecter of tradition.

Of course the President's opponents immediately dubbed rotation a "spoils system" in which political hacks would replace experienced and intelligent bureaucrats. But Jackson dismissed this criticism as a mere ruse to disguise the horror that aristocrats felt about popular elections. "*Every* officer should in his turn pass before the people, for their approval or rejection," he told George Bancroft at a later date. In declaring his desire to change the Constitution so that the people directly elected the President, Jackson was setting a tone which the Democratic party would imitate and repeat throughout this era: namely, their faith and confidence in the ability of the people to govern themselves. Jacksonians always preached the fundamental principle that the people were good, trustworthy, and capable of self-rule. And since the people can govern themselves and had a right to select their chief executive, "let us, then," Jackson told the Congress, "amend our system" to allow "the fair expression of the will of the majority."

"The will of the majority." Those words carried great weight with Andrew Jackson. Other men, including many of the Founding Fathers, were apprehensive about majority will. After all, the majority might tyrannize the minority. Then what? But such worries did not trouble Jackson. He understood the danger but felt there was no other means of protecting liberty. "The people are sovereign," he insisted, "their will is absolute." If the people can not be trusted then the Republic will fall. But Old Hickory trusted the people implicitly and felt the Union was safe so long as those in government not only relied on the people and respected them but had faith in them and treated them as equals.

Jackson also advocated what he called "the right of instruction," namely the right of the people to instruct their representatives as to their will. In other words when the people formally and legally expressed their wishes, such as might be done in a convention or an election, then their representatives, whether in Congress or the state legislatures, were bound to respect those wishes by carrying them out or resigning their office. Jackson did not expect the electorate to regularly or constantly interfere in the governmental process. Only those issues of major importance or concern would stir them into action. But on those occasions when they did stir themselves, then the representatives *must* defer to the popular will or step aside and allow someone else to take their place. Such a practice would insure the continued development of a democratic society, he said.

The "constant celebration" of the people, then, is fundamental to any understanding of Jacksonian Democracy. And it was that celebration that gave the era its distinctive quality. As Alexis de Tocqueville wrote in his classic work, *Democracy in America:* "The people reign in the American political world, as the Deity does in the universe. They are the cause and aim of all things; everything comes from them, and everything is absorbed in them."

The advent of democracy in America was closely associated with Andrew Jackson because of his repeated declarations about the virtue and sovereignty of the people, as well as his opposition to elitism and aristocracy. Jackson made exaggerated claims for majoritarian rule, advocating a system whereby, as he said, "*every* officer should in his turn pass before the people, for their approval or rejection," including federal judges, legislators, and chief executives. His rather advanced democratic program has yet to be achieved. Still his enthusiasm and faith in the people fixed the standard by which democratic progress in the United States can be measured.

Indeed, Jackson was far ahead of his time in his commitment to popular self-government. He still is. His ideas probably can never be implemented in a country of such heterogeneity and geographical expanse as the United States. Nevertheless, his populist creed, his populist enthusiasm, his populist cries and shouts, continue to inspire political leaders as well as generate the kind of excitement and support among the electorate that frequently result in progressive reforms that benefit the entire country.

In his own lifetime Jackson served more as a symbol of the arrival of democracy in America than as a true instigator of its rise to political preeminence. Democracy had been rising for decades, nurtured in large measure by the admission of new states which provided universal white manhood suffrage and completely eliminated all vestiges of privilege with regard to voting or holding public office. More important, by the 1830s, a large number of people expected to exercise a greater voice in their government.

With an expanding economy so characteristic of the Jacksonian era, increased social mobility, rising expectations, and a higher standard of living, the electorate felt more confident in asserting their political rights and in demanding a sympathetic response from their government.

It cannot be denied that strong elements of democracy were embedded in the governmental system established by the Founding Fathers in the Constitution, such as the conviction that legitimate government exists by virtue of the consent of the governed. But they established a government of checks and balances, such as the electoral college and an appointed Supreme Court, to prevent, among other things, some of the dangers inherent in a completely democratic system. It was a republican form of government the Founders erected, not a democratic one. In the *Federalist* no. 10, James Madison wrote that "democracies have ever been spectacles of turbulence and contention; have ever been found incompatible with personal security or the rights of property; and have in general been as short in their lives as they have been violent in their deaths."

Nevertheless, by the close of the Jacksonian age political commentators were no longer talking about republicanism. Instead they spoke solely in terms of democracy. Madison's gloomy views had been forgotten. John L. O'Sullivan, in an essay he wrote for the *Democratic Review*, discussed the development and significance of democracy in shaping the course of American history without once mentioning republicanism. By the close of the Jacksonian era the notions of the Founding Fathers about republicanism had been completely replaced by the doctrines of democracy, even though the form of government still retained virtually all of its original republican features.

Still, this Jacksonian age had a long way to go before it would completely understand or practice the most basic tenets of democracy. The Jacksonians spoke of equality and meant it. But equality did not apply to blacks or Indians or women. Not that they should be faulted for failing to recognize what the twentieth century holds as the meaning and application of the term. They simply had no conception of what modern Americans understand by equality and democracy. For the most part they did not think about blacks or Indians or women when they spoke of the suffrage. It probably never crossed their minds. When they talked about "the people" they meant—in political terms—white males over the age of twenty-one.

Nor did they fully comprehend the meaning of civil rights. (Most probably Americans of the twentieth century—that is, prior to the 1950s—did not comprehend it either.) Jackson himself was deficient in this regard, and he ran into a thicket of legal, constitutional, and political problems because of it. An important example of these problems occurred near the end of his second term in office.

On July 30, 1835, abolitionist literature sent through the mails was seized by an angry mob in Charleston, South Carolina, and burned. This mob presumed the right to censor the mail. Jackson believed that the mail must be delivered. But he also believed that abolitionist literature fomented race riots. He called the literature "unconstitutional and wicked." But who should decide the question? Surely what South Carolina regarded as inflammatory might be vastly different from what Massachusetts might find explosive. Did a sender have the right to mail his propaganda to whomever he wished? But what of the right of the receiver to be spared the offense or embarrassment of receiving objectionable literature? And there were other questions.

Jackson went to the Congress because he believed the national legislature had the right to control the mails in order to protect public safety. Men like John C. Calhoun and many other southerners felt the Congress should forbid delivery of any material in any state or territory where local law outlawed such material. But the Congress refused to oblige either Jackson or Calhoun and passed the Post Office Act of 1836, which forbade local postmasters from interfering with the delivery of the mail. Nevertheless, southerners regularly violated this law on the assumption that federal authority over the mail ceased at the reception point. As William Leggett, editor of the New York *Evening Post*, declared: "If the government once begins to discriminate as to what is orthodox and what heterodox in opinion, what is safe and what unsafe in tendency, farewell, a long farewell to our freedom." A future attorney general later decided in 1857 that a postmaster may refuse to deliver what he regards as incendiary but it is up to the courts to decide in due course what is and what is not incendiary.

Jackson also used federal troops to break a strike. He is the first President to respond to a labor dispute in this manner. When violence flared on the Chesapeake and Ohio Canal near Williamsport, Maryland, in mid-January 1834, and the governor of the state asked Jackson for military assistance, the President responded by directing the Secretary of War to order "such military as will be able to aid the civil authority of Maryland to put down the riotous assembly." Jackson responded to his perceived duty to maintain law and order, especially when the governor appealed for aid. He felt he must protect the rights of the community and the nation.

But the issue that caused Jackson the most difficulty and greatest concern, and yet impacted tremendously on the question of democracy, was his war against the Second National Bank of the United States (BUS). The Bank was chartered by the federal government in 1816 with a capital stock of $35 million, of which one-fifth was purchased by the government and the remaining four-fifths sold to the public. The government's funds were deposited in the BUS and the Bank served as an agent in the collection and transmittal of taxes. The government was not charged for this service.

The BUS was headquartered on Chestnut Street in Philadelphia and established twenty-six branches throughout the country. It was run by a board of directors, five of whom were appointed by the government of the United States and twenty elected by the public stockholders. Actually, the affairs of the Bank were managed by a president chosen by the stockholders. At the time Jackson initiated his war, Nicholas Biddle, a well-educated, intelligent scion of a wealthy and socially prominent Philadelphia family, served as president.

Born in 1786, the son of a successful merchant who had served in the Revolution, Biddle entered the University of Pennsylvania at the age of ten and completed all the requirements for a degree within three years. But because of his youth, the university refused to grant the degree. So Biddle enrolled at Princeton and in 1801, at the age of fifteen, received his bachelor's degree and gave the valedictory address. After that he toured Europe and was so taken by the art and architecture of Greece that upon his return to the United States he helped introduce classical architecture in this country and was an important contributor to the Greek Revival. He studied law, won election to the Pennsylvania legislature, and demonstrated such a sophisticated understanding of the operation of the BUS that on January 7, 1823, he was elected its president.

A brilliant administrator, the prototype of the modern business executive, Biddle transformed what was essentially a nationwide branch-banking system, with authority to act as a federal fiscal agent, into a genuine central bank. And a central bank, by definition, is an institution acting as an agent of the government, in this case the federal government, that has the power to create and destroy the circulating media. Biddle efficiently controlled the circulating media and later demonstrated that he could even initiate a financial panic.

Jackson's dislike of the BUS was rooted in his hatred for speculation and paper money generally, a hatred that resulted from a number of bad experiences as a young man, when he almost landed in debtor's prison. He objected to the paper-issuing, credit-producing aspects of banking and at one point actually told Biddle that "I do not dislike your Bank any more than all banks." Also he came to believe that the BUS threatened individual liberty. He claimed that the Bank intruded into the political process to arrange the election of persons who were friendly to the Bank and its interests. He was convinced that BUS money had been used against him in the election of 1828. Moreover, he felt the institution served the interests of the wealthy classes at the expense of the average citizen. Since the federal government placed all its deposits in the BUS—deposits representing the taxes of all—the interest

earned on the deposits was not shared by taxpayers but went instead to the stockholders.

Jackson turned to the Congress with his complaints and asked
it to look into the problem. He said that the BUS had failed to provide sound credit and currency—which was absurd—and needed
legislative fixing. At this point the President most probably would
have accepted amendments to the Bank's charter, but as events developed he finally determined to "kill the monster," as he called
the BUS, and save the people from its corrupting influence.

What changed Jackson's mind was the decision of Biddle—
prodded by Henry Clay—to request a recharter of the Bank four
years before the present charter expired. The request was politically motivated. It would supposedly place Jackson in an awkward
position: either to sign a recharter bill in which Biddle would get
what he wanted, or veto it, in which case Henry Clay could challenge Jackson before the people in the next presidential election.
Both Biddle and Clay were convinced that the American people
would never permit the destruction of the BUS and would unseat
Jackson and replace him with Clay. Then, as President, Clay
would sign a new rechartering bill.

Jackson immediately recognized this political plot. In his
mind it convinced him totally that what he had been saying about
the Bank being a threat to liberty was true. Roger B. Taney, the Attorney General, stated the situation precisely: "Now as I understand the application at the present time, it means in plain English
this—the Bank says to the President, your next election is at
hand—if you charter us, well—if not, beware of your power." But
Jackson would never yield to such threats. "I will prove to them
that I never flinch," he raged, "that they were mistaken when they
expect to act upon me by such circumstances."

In January 1832, a bill for recharter was introduced into Congress and by July had passed both houses. Biddle was delighted. "I
congratulate our friends most cordially upon the most satisfactory
result," he wrote. "Now for the President." And the President was
waiting. When Martin Van Buren came to the White House to see
Jackson he found the old man lying on a couch, gasping for
breath. As Van Buren entered the room Jackson glanced up, his

face aglow, and he seized his friend's hand. "The bank, Mr. Van Buren, is trying to kill me," he said. Then, pressing Van Buren's hand tightly, he added, *"but I will kill it."*

A ringing veto message was sent down to the Congress on July 10, 1832. It had been written by a number of members of his Kitchen Cabinet*, particularly Amos Kendall, Roger B. Taney, Andrew Jackson Donelson (Jackson's nephew and personal secretary), Levi Woodbury and, of course, Jackson himself. It was one of the most important presidential vetoes in constitutional history, for in it Jackson cited all manner of reasons for killing the bill, not simply the constitutional reason, as was customary. All previous presidential vetoes were based on a constitutional disagreement. Indeed, it was generally believed that such a disagreement was the only ground for a veto. Jackson thought otherwise. He gave political, social, and economic reasons for his disapproval. He said the Bank had been granted monopoly privileges that created inequities. In the United States, he felt, there must be equality for all. No special advantages for anyone or any corporate institution. He said the BUS was a threat to the nation's free electoral process and its democratic system of government. And it earned money for foreign investors from the taxes collected from all Americans. He challenged the finding of the Supreme Court about the Bank's constitutionality and told the Congress they must decide for themselves the constitutionality of whatever bill comes before them, just as he, the President, must also do. John Marshall in his majority decision in the case *McCulloch* v. *Maryland* agreed with Alexander Hamilton's contention that Congress possessed implied power to carry out its enumerated responsibilities as well as power that were "necessary and proper" to accomplish a legitimate end within the scope of the Constitution. Acting under its implied powers the Congress had every right to establish a national bank,

---

* The term "Kitchen Cabinet" was invented by Jackson's political enemies. It referred to a group of the President's friends and associates outside the official (or "Parlor") Cabinet who supposedly slipped into Jackson's study in the White House by way of the back stairs through the kitchen to advise him on the running of the government and the Democratic party.

Marshall decreed. Moreover, he declared that states did not have the right to tax an agency of the federal government, contending that "the power to tax involves the power to destroy."

Jackson disagreed with the Supreme Court on the constitutional right of Congress to establish a bank. "To this conclusion I cannot assent," he said. The Congress and the President "must each for itself be guided by its own opinion of the Constitution. It is as much the duty of the house of Representatives, of the Senate, and of the President to decide upon the constitutionality of any bill or resolution which may be presented to them for passage or approval as it is of the supreme judges when it may be brought before them for judicial decision. The opinion of the judges has no more authority over Congress than the opinion of Congress has over the judges, and on that point the President is independent of both. The authority of the Supreme Court must not, therefore, be permitted to control the Congress or the Executive when acting in their legislative capacities, but to have only such influence as the force of their reasoning may deserve."

He closed the message with this explosive statement:

It is to be regretted that the rich and powerful too often bend the acts of government to their selfish purposes. Distinctions in society will always exist under every just government. Equality of talents, of education, or of wealth can not be produced by human institutions. In the full enjoyment of the gifts of Heaven and the fruits of superior industry, economy, and virtue, every man is equally entitled to protection by law; but when the laws undertake to add to these natural and just advantages artificial distinctions, to grant titles, gratuities, and exclusive privileges, to make the rich richer and the potent more powerful, the humble members of society—the farmers, mechanics, and laborers—who have neither the time nor the means of securing like favors to themselves, have a right to complain of the injustice of their Government. There are no necessary evils in government. Its evils exist only in its abuses. If it would confine itself to equal protection, and, as Heaven does its rains, shower its favors alike on the high and the low, the rich and the poor, it would be an unqualified blessing. In the act before me there seems to be a wide and unnecessary departure from these just principles.

The implications of Jackson's veto were tremendous—and any number of Americans spotted them immediately. For the Presi-

dent placed the Congress on notice that he was assuming legislative power with them. Before passing any bill in the future, both
houses of Congress must first check with the President to see if he
has any objection to it, otherwise they risk a veto. Since the President can invalidate a law for any ostensible reason, it behooved the
Congress to gain his prior consent before proceeding with any legislation.

Friends of the BUS were flabbergasted by Jackson's claims. It
was a "manifesto of anarchy," Nicholas Biddle angrily insisted,
"such as Marat or Robespierre might have issued to the mobs"
during the French Revolution. Senator Daniel Webster was more
specific. Jackson "claims for the President, not the power of approval," he thundered, "but the primary power of originating
laws." Senator Henry Clay agreed. The action of the President, he
protested, "was a pervasion of the veto power." An unfriendly
newspaper went further. "The true power of this government," edi-
torialized the Washington *National Intelligencer,* "*ought* to be to
lie in the Congress of the United States. . . . It was never contem-
plated that its deliberately expressed opinions should be lightly
disregarded—its well considered acts repeatedly rejected—and its
legal authority overtopped by another and differently constituted
power." But that was what Jackson was doing and, of course, he
did it in the name of the people. "Congress is the *democratic*
branch of the government," shrilled the *National Intelligencer,* not
the executive. "If power is safe anywhere in a Republic it is safe
with the representatives."

Obviously, Jackson thought otherwise. He believed that the
President was the direct representative of all the people and responsible to them. And he said so later in a special message to the
Senate. He believed he was the head of the government, the first
among equals. He was in charge because he was elected by all the
people and therefore served as their spokesman and tribune.

"We have arrived at a new epoch," warned Senator Webster.
"We are entering on experiments with the government and the
Constitution, hitherto untried, and of fearful and appalling aspect."
And so it seemed to most of the opposition. They had indeed ar-
rived at a new epoch, one which acknowledged the right of the
majority to exercise control in the operation of government, one in

which the chief executive, elected by the people, directed the affairs of the nation and served as head of state.

After Jackson won reelection in 1832 over Henry Clay he decided to kill the "hydra-headed monster" immediately by withdrawing the government's deposits from the BUS. When his Secretary of the Treasury refused to carry out this decision and refused to resign, Jackson fired him, again creating an important precedent. Jackson was the first President to dismiss a cabinet officer. Previous Presidents had nudged obstreperous secretaries into resigning. It was generally assumed that since cabinet positions had been created by Congress and appointments to it required the approval of the Senate that dismissal also required the consent of the upper house. This was especially true of the Treasury post because the Congress controlled the purse strings and the Secretary of the Treasury was obliged to report to the legislature, not to the chief executive. Even so, Jackson believed and determined once and for all that the President had complete control over all members of the cabinet, which meant, of course, that it not only gave him total control over the executive branch of the government but also extra leverage in dispersing the nation's finances.

The Senate struggled long and hard to prevent Jackson from removing the deposits—actually he did not remove them in one fell swoop but rather drew them out as needed to operate the government, while new funds were placed in selected state banks, called "pet" banks, in the principal cities. Biddle foolishly responded by demonstrating the full power of the Bank to bring economic havoc to the country. He directed a general curtailment of loans throughout the entire banking system. He refused to increase discounts and restricted discounted bills of exchange to 90 days. Western branch banks were ordered to purchase bills of exchange payable solely in eastern cities. "This worthy President thinks that because he has scalped Indians and imprisoned Judges, he is to have his way with the Bank. He is mistaken." Biddle's squeeze pitched the country into an economic recession during the winter of 1833–34 and frightened many people into believing the President's policy toward the Second National Bank had produced nothing but catastrophe. "Damn your old soul," wrote one outraged Jackson opponent from Cincinnati, "remove them deposites back again, and recharter the bank, or you will certainly be shot in less than two weeks and that by myself!!!" But Jackson would not yield. When business men came to the White House to beg him to save them from their financial plight the President responded: "What do you come to me for? Go to Nicholas Biddle. We have no money here. Biddle has all the money. He has millions of specie in his vaults, at this moment, lying idle, and yet you come to me to save you from breaking." And to Martin Van Buren, Jackson said: "I am ready with the screws to draw every tooth" in the head of the monster, "and then the stumps."

The President rightly guessed that the American people would at last understand how much power Biddle and his Bank exercised over their lives and how arbitrarily that power could be used to blackmail their government into submission. They turned away from "Czar Nick," as the Democrats called him, with disgust. Eventually the House of Representatives passed a series of resolutions condemning the BUS for calling in loans and attempting to win recharter through economic pressure. These resolutions specifically stated that rechartering should be denied, that the deposits should be kept with the pets, and that a special committee should investigate the Bank's affairs and learn the reasons for the financial panic that had been loosed upon the country. That spelled the end of the Bank. "The Bank is dead," one cabinet officer exulted. "I have obtained a glorious triumph," cried Andrew Jackson when he heard what the House had done. The vote "has put to death that mamouth of corruption and power, the Bank of the United States."

Basically the Bank War was a power struggle, a political battle between Andrew Jackson—and everything he represented in terms of democratic government—and Nicholas Biddle and his pro-Bank allies, who were concerned for the financial stability and future growth of the country. At stake was whether this nation could survive as a democracy if private, unaccountable concentrations of wealth are more powerful than a democratically elected government. When it became clear to the American people what was involved, they rallied in support of Jackson's position. And this essential meaning of the Bank War has influenced progressives and reformers throughout American history. For it happens again and again that individuals and groups will attempt to use the government to advance their own special interests even if it injures the people.

Another important effect of the Bank War was the way in which it altered the relationship between the electorate and the chief executive. The Jacksonian concept that the President is the only elective officer of the national government who represents all the people was reemphasized and strengthened. Congressmen represented states or fragments of states. But the President, according to Jackson, had a wider responsibility. His constituency as President cut across all states, sections, classes, and economic divisions and encompassed the entire mass of the American people. Earlier Presidents had nowhere to turn when they locked horns with Congress because they lacked a national power base to fall back on for support. They lacked a national constituency. They tended, therefore, to act like prime ministers in the British fashion. But Jackson changed that. He led the way in creating a national political base on which presidential power could rest securely. When he decreed the destruction of the BUS and the Congress sought to thwart his intentions, he simply turned to the country at large and asked the people for their support. That was the first time in American history that a major issue had been taken directly to the people for decision. When the electorate responded in 1832 by defeating Clay's presidential candidacy so decisively, Jackson was able to claim a mandate and proceed to slay "the monster Bank," despite fierce Congressional objections. Presidential power had been buttressed by mass support. The executive office was never quite the same again.

The destruction of the BUS terminated central banking in the United States until the passage of the Federal Reserve system during the administration of Woodrow Wilson. State banks now enjoyed a great deal of freedom and unfortunately began to issue millions of dollars of paper money, something Jackson hated with a passion. In order to put a curb on this inflation of the currency he issued his Specie Circular in 1836, which required gold and silver for the purchase of land from the government. Here was another demonstration of executive power undertaken without the consent or the knowledge of the Congress. Here was a clear indication of the arrival of an imperial presidency. Still the flood of paper released by the state banks helped to sustain and augment the industrial growth and expansion that so characterized the Jacksonian years. It produced a galvanic force that marked the emergence of a new and more powerful industrial society.

But, less than two weeks after Jackson left the White House and turned the presidency over to his successor, Martin Van Buren, the country suffered a major financial collapse. On March 17, 1837, I. and L. Joseph of New York, one of the largest dealers in domestic exchanges, went bankrupt. What brought this about was the failure of the New Orleans cotton market, triggered by a reduction in purchases by British buyers, and since the I. and L. Joseph Company had extensive dealings with a variety of commercial and mercantile enterprises, as well as banks, its bankruptcy set off a chain reaction that pulled down dozens of other companies. The price of specie rose and created a run on the banks, forcing a suspension of specie payments by the banks. Over the next several months hundreds of bankruptcies occurred. The nation seemed on the verge of total financial disaster.

But the Panic of 1837 was a worldwide depression and actually had nothing to do with Jackson's killing of the Second National Bank or his Specie Circular. Perhaps the killing of the Bank and the issuance of the Circular were detrimental to the general economic health of the nation, but in themselves they did not cause the onset of the panic. President Van Buren spent his entire administration trying to cope with the depression and finally won passage of the Independent Treasury—a "divorce" or subtreasury plan—which required the public money to be managed by the government itself without the assistance of banks. Deposits would be "stored" in subtreasury buildings in the major cities around the country and withdrawn as needed by the government. In this way no private agency could profit from the use of public funds.

This Independent Treasury system was repealed in the John Tyler administration but resurrected during the administration of James Knox Polk, and it remained the basic system for the collection, safekeeping, transfer, and disbursement of the government's money until it was replaced in the twentieth century by the Federal Reserve System.

In the minds of many Jacksonians one benefit resulting from the destruction of the Second National Bank was the boost it gave to developing democracy within the country. The Bank was regarded as the instrument of the rich, and indeed much of the rhetoric against the Bank was the argument that the BUS robbed the poor to favor the wealthy. Thus the Democratic party came to rest on a moral base at the very beginning of its existence, citing its war against the BUS as evidence of its concern for the welfare of the ordinary citizen against powerful moneyed interests who will use their money to bribe the government to advance and protect their greedy purposes. This populistic stance was one of the more important contributions by the Jacksonians to the future course and direction of American political history. Lobbyists of one kind or another will always try to promote special interests but as Jackson declared in his veto message, care must be taken that government "confine itself to equal protection, and, as Heaven does its rains, shower its favors alike on the high and the low, the rich and the poor." In his Farewell Address he added: "Justice—full and ample justice—to every portion of the United States . . . should guide the deliberations of every public body, whether it be State or national."

At one point in his career Jackson himself made a stab at defining what historians would later call Jacksonian Democracy. He said that if the "virtuous yeomanry" wished to distinguish true Democrats from "Whiggs, nullies [nullifiers] & blue light federalists [New Englanders who allegedly signaled the British fleet during the War of 1812 with blue lights to indicate a safe haven]" all they had to do was "enquire of them, are you opposed to a national

Bank—are you in favor of a strict construction of the federal and State constitution—are you in favor of rotation in office—do you subscribe to the republican rule that the people are the sovereign power, the officers their agents, and that upon all national or general subjects, as well as local, they have a right to instruct their agents & representatives, and they are bound to obey or resign—in short are they true republicans agreeable to the true Jeffersonian creed."

Again, in his Farewell Address, he summed up the idea of Jacksonian Democracy in a single sentence. "To you," he told the American people, "everyone placed in authority is ultimately responsible." If all Americans will stay watchful and jealous of their rights, if the people remain "uncorrupted and incorruptible," then the nation is safe and "the cause of freedom will continue to triumph over all its enemies."

Over the years and down to the present day Jacksonian Democracy continues to exert great appeal to the American people because it asserts in the most forceful and compelling manner the right of all the people to self-government. Its populistic cry, its populistic creed, its populistic fervor were unique for its time, and they have admirably served succeeding generations of Americans in their efforts to bring reforms and improvements to the political system. Democracy will continue to flourish in this country as long as that cry and that creed and that fervor endure.

CHAPTER THREE

Indian Removal

Andrew Jackson took particular pride in solving—at least to his mind it was a solution—the problem of the Indians. He had long advocated their removal west of the Mississippi River, and it was one of his most cherished goals on becoming President.

The idea of Indian removal goes back several decades and probably originated with Thomas Jefferson. Jackson favored it for several reasons: to protect the American people and provide greater security for the United States; and to prevent the certain annihilation of Indian life and culture that would occur if the tribes were to remain within eastern states. The opportunity to obtain the rich lands occupied by the Native Americans in the south also figured into his thinking. By the time Old Hickory came to lead his Tennessee volunteers against the Creek Nation in 1813 he had pretty much decided what must be done to resolve the question of the presence of the Indian. The Creeks had been driven to raise their tomahawks against white settlers at Fort Mims in October, 1811, when Tecumseh, the great Shawnee leader, came down from

Detroit and visited the Creek Nation in Alabama and stirred once again the old hatreds between the white and red men.

"Let the white race perish!" Tecumseh stormed. "They seize your land; they corrupt your women; they trample on the bones of your dead! Back where they came, upon a trail of blood, they must be driven! Back—aye, back to the great water whose accursed waves brought them to our shores! Burn their dwellings —destroy their stock—slay their wives and children, that the very breed may perish. War now! War always! War on the living! War on the dead!"

One of the Creek chiefs protested this maniacal outburst and warned against invoking the wrath of the white man. Tecumseh, in a rage, thrust a finger into the face of the chief and uttered a fearful vow. "Your blood is white. . . . You do not believe the Great Spirit sent me. You shall believe it. I will leave directly and go straight to Detroit. When I get there I will stamp my foot upon the ground and shake down every house in Tookabatcha."

Weeks later it happened, just as Tecumseh had vowed. The earth began to rumble and shake, and every house in Tookabatcha toppled to the ground. The people scurried about in a state of bewilderment and terror. "Tecumseh has got to Detroit," they cried. "We feel the shake of his foot."

The unusual earthquake that occurred in the Mississippi Valley at that moment seemed like a divine call to arms, and not much later the Creeks signaled the start of war by massacring the settlers at Fort Mims in southern Alabama. But not all the Creeks joined the war. Many assisted Jackson and his Tennessee volunteers in defeating the hostile Creeks, or Red Sticks, as they were frequently called on account of their practice of painting their war clubs a bright red color. Thus, when the war ended with the Battle of Horseshoe Bend on March 27, 1814, and Jackson imposed as the principal condition for peace the surrender of 23 million acres of land to the United States, the friendly Creeks protested. Such a huge indemnity punished not only the Red Sticks but the entire Creek Nation. Indeed, it was not punishment that Jackson was inflicting on the

Creeks but annihilation. In a moving appeal, the friendly Indians reminded Jackson of the dangers they had shared and of their loyalty and support throughout the war. In response, Sharp Knife, as the Indians frequently called Old Hickory, reminded them of Tecumseh's visit and how the chief had been allowed to incite the young Creek warriors to raise the tomahawk against American settlers. When the friendly Creeks replied that most of them did not respond to his call and that in any event they were powerless to stop him, Jackson stood his ground. He showed little compassion for their plight. "You should have seized him instantly and sent him as a prisoner to your Great Father in Washington," he responded. "Or, cut his throat."

The treaty imposed was indeed a cruel punishment, but Jackson felt justified because the Creeks had jeopardized the safety and security of the United States by launching their attack at a time when his country was locked in a deadly struggle with Great Britain. Unfortunately for the hostile Indians, they moved too quickly in raising the tomahawk. Had they waited and synchronized their war with the British invasion at New Orleans in 1814 they might have changed the outcome of the entire conflict along the Gulf coastline. Fortunately for the United States, the Indians jumped the gun and paid a frightful price.

In subsequent years, Jackson, on assignment from the President as Indian treaty commissioner, reminded other southern tribes what had happened to the Creeks and what might happen to them if they did not obey him. And at each one of his meetings with the tribes he demanded the surrender of their land in exchange for land beyond the Mississippi River. So certain had he become by this time that removal was the only answer to the Indian problem that upon election as President he gave the enactment of a removal bill the highest priority. And despite keen opposition among some members of Congress from both houses, a Removal Act was passed on May 28, 1830. It was the first major piece of legislation of Jackson's administration.

The Removal Act of 1830 provided funds for negotiating with the Five Civilized Tribes—the Creeks, Cherokees, Choctaws,

Chickasaws, and Seminoles—and relocating them in the west. An Indian Territory would be established—it later became the state of Oklahoma—in which each tribe could function independently and without interference from the United States. Treaties would be signed in which the southern Indians would surrender all their land in the east and receive in return an equivalent amount of land in the west. In addition, they would be provided transportation, food, and some tools. A number of tribes easily submitted to the command of the "Great Father" in Washington and surrendered their lands without a fight. But others resisted. The most notable was the Cherokee Nation, a very "civilized" tribe, boasting schools, a written language, a newspaper, and a constitution. The Cherokees took their complaint to the U.S. Supreme Court.

What they did was to sue the state of Georgia for attempting to impose its laws over the Cherokee Nation. Jackson and the Georgians contended that the Indians were subject to state law; the Indians believed they constituted an independent and sovereign nation and therefore were not subject to state law. In his decision in the case *Cherokee Nation* v. *Georgia*, Chief Justice John Marshall ruled that the Indians were not subject to state law, but went on to state that they were not independent either. They were wards of the federal government; in effect, "domestic dependents."

Nowhere does the Constitution give specific authority to the federal government to treat with the Indians. However, it was generally assumed that the treaty clause provided that authority. But in requiring treaties to obtain land from the tribes did that not indicate that the Indian tribes were independent powers? that they were sovereign nations? Not according to Marshall. They were, he said, "domestic dependent nations in a state of pupilage"—whatever that meant. Despite the Marshall decision, it should be noted that the United States government until 1871 maintained the legal fiction that the tribes were indeed independent nations. From 1778, when the first treaty with the Indians was signed, to 1871, when the last one was concluded by the United States, all 370 treaties, with one exception, took the position that Indian titles to their lands could only be extinguished through the signing of treaties, just as was done with foreign nations. Legal right to their land was also recognized.

So the Cherokees refused to submit to Georgia law. For its part, Georgia boycotted the legal proceedings and refused to acknowledge the right of the Supreme Court to direct its actions. In December 1830, the legislature prohibited white men from entering Indian territory after March 1, 1831, without permission from the state. This law was meant to keep missionaries from inciting the Indians to resist obeying Georgia law. As a consequence a dozen missionaries were arrested and placed in custody, but most of them accepted pardons from the governor on condition that they would cease violating Georgia law. However, Samuel A. Worcester and Dr. Elizur Butler refused the condition and were remanded to prison. They sued for their freedom and in the case *Worcester* v. *Georgia*, the Supreme Court again ruled against Georgia and ordered the state not to interfere. The state's superior court was instructed to reverse its previous ruling against the missionaries. The Supreme Court then adjourned.

When he heard the *Worcester* decision, Jackson supposedly said: "Well, John Marshall has made his decision: *now, let him enforce it!*" It is unlikely that Jackson came up with so pithy a retort to the decision for the simple reason that there was nothing to enforce. The Supreme Court had adjourned after invalidating the Georgia law and ordering the state's superior court to reverse itself. Not until the state defied the decision and the Supreme Court either summoned state officials to appear before it for contempt for refusing to obey its order or issued a writ of habeas corpus for the release of the two missionaries was there anything more the federal government could do. According to the Judiciary Act of 1789, the high court could issue an order of compliance only when a case had been remanded without response. Since the Court had adjourned and would not reconvene for practically an entire year, action in winning the release of the two men came to a complete halt. Jackson was under no obligation to act. Moreover, there is some question as to whether the Court could interfere in freeing Worcester and Butler. The existing habeas corpus law did not apply in this case since the missionaries had been imprisoned by state authorities, not federal authorities. Jackson's reaction to the decision was not defiance, as expressed in the quotation attributed to him, but wait-and-see, the clear recognition that the ruling hung suspended in time. This explains why he wrote to General John Coffee that "the decision of the supreme court has fell still born, and they find that it cannot coerce Georgia to yield to its mandate."

What must be remembered in understanding Jackson's position in this dispute was that at this very time the crisis over nullification with South Carolina was gathering momentum and threatened to trigger violence and civil war. The last thing the President wanted during the nullification danger was a confrontation with Georgia. He therefore acted with caution in maneuvering Georgia away from a defiant stance at the same time he faced down the nullifiers in South Carolina. Eventually he pressured the Georgia governor into freeing the missionaries at the same time that the Cherokees were urged by their friends in Congress to remove. Even Justice John McLean, who concurred in the *Worcester* decision, advised a Cherokee delegation in Washington to sign a removal treaty. And William Wirt, who represented the Cherokee Nation before the Supreme Court, agreed not to make any further motions before the high court. On January 14, 1833, the missionaries were released and the danger of a confrontation with Georgia evaporated.

President Jackson met with the Principal Chief of the Cherokee Nation, John Ross, in the White House on February 5, 1834. Ross was a Scot with only a dash of Cherokee blood in his veins— one-eighth to be precise. Jackson cordially disliked the Principal Chief and called him "a great villain" because he had actively and persistently thwarted the President's determination to remove the Indians beyond the Mississippi River. Jackson much preferred to deal with Major Ridge, his son John Ridge, Elias Boudinot, the editor of the Cherokee *Phoenix*, and his brother, Stand Watie, who understood his determination to expel the Cherokees from their eastern lands. The Principal Chief had come to the White House to forestall the "Great Father" from dispatching the Reverend John F.

Schermerhorn, a scheming and ambitious cleric, to the Cherokee Nation to work out a treaty with the Ridge faction. After all, he, John Ross, was the Principal Chief and he had a right to oversee the negotiations. But the President suspected his motives. Ross "often proposed to make a treaty for mony alone," said Jackson, "& not Land." At one point in their discussion the Chief demanded $20 million plus indemnification for past treaty violations. Jackson rejected the demand as ridiculous and accused Ross of trifling with him. He was convinced that the Chief cared nothing for the welfare of his people. Ross's only concern, according to the President, was his economic self-interest and the interest of the other "half breeds" who supported his "preposterous" demands. Like the Bank supporters, Ross and his allies, according to Jackson, constituted an elite class intent on centralizing tribal power to gain further economic advantages at the expense of the entire Cherokee Nation.

At length, with the assistance of the Ridge Treaty party, the Reverend Schermerhorn extracted a treaty—the Treaty of New Echota—by which the Cherokees ceded to the United States all their lands east of the Mississippi River in return for $4.5 million and an equivalent amount of land in the Indian Territory. A removal program was also spelled out by which payments for subsistence, blankets, kettles, rifles, and the like, were provided. Removal was to begin within two years from the ratification of the treaty.

Through fraud and chicanery the Treaty of New Echota was approved by the Cherokee Nation by the incredibly small vote of 79 to 7. Not much later Congress received petitions signed by over 14,000 Cherokees protesting the treaty. Congress turned a deaf ear. By a vote of 31 to 15 the Senate of the United States narrowly ratified the treaty. Actual removal was therefore to begin on May 23, 1838.

The Cherokees had two years to prepare for the exodus, but instead of accepting the determination of the President to get rid of them, as the Ridge party had done, the Indians listened to the Principal Chief, who urged that they resist the execution of the treaty to the bitter end in some fanciful hope that Jackson and Congress might change their minds and allow them to stay where they were. For two years the Cherokees remained in their homes, depending on Ross to find a way to spare them the pain of moving from everything they held dear. Ross was as determined as Jackson to have his own way. Only the President, as it turned out, had greater resources and greater determination.

When the time finally ran out and the deadline for the evacuation was reached the Cherokees were totally unprepared for what awaited them. And what happened was criminal. The authorities in Georgia were itching to get their hands on these recalcitrant "redskins." The militia was immediately dispatched to the Cherokee lands to round up the Indians. And these soldiers were not disposed to treat their victims with anything other than contempt and a total disregard for their personal well-being. Stockades were hastily erected "for gathering in and holding the Indians preparatory to removal." These concentration camps—for surely that is what they were—initiated the horror that awaited the Cherokees on their long journey to the west. The stockades became armed forts from which the militia sallied forth in search of victims wherever they might be hiding. Indian families in their cabins and houses at dinner were "startled by the sudden gleam of bayonets in the doorway and rose up to be driven with blows and oaths along the weary miles of trail which led to the stockade. Men were seized in their fields, women were taken from their wheels and children from their play." When the captured Cherokees turned for one last look at their homes they frequently saw them in flames, set ablaze by the looters who followed the soldiers and scavenged for whatever items of worth they could find among the belongings of the Indians. Cattle was stolen, graves desecrated, fields burned. Said one Georgia militiaman who later served in the Confederate army: "I fought through the Civil War and have seen men shot to pieces and slaughtered by thousands, but the Cherokee removal was the cruelest I ever saw."

It was reported that within a single week the efficient Georgians rounded up over 1,700 hapless Cherokees. Homeless and destitute, these frightened and bewildered Indians were herded into the stockades, where many of them sickened and died. "Oh! the misery and wretchedness that presents itself to our view in going among these people," wrote one man. The sight seared itself forever in his memory. By June the survivors were ready to be transported to the west. In the first contingent 1,000 Cherokees were taken by steamboats down the Tennessee River, then boxed like cattle into railroad cars, and finally sent along a trail the Indians came to call "The Trail of Tears" to their final destination in the Indian Territory. It was an 800-mile journey of sickness, misery, and death. About 18,000 Cherokees were removed in this manner, of whom 4,000 died along the way.

Some white men tried to spare the Cherokees this agony. General Winfield Scott, who commanded the federal part of this operation, ordered his men to treat the Indians with decency and understanding. He also delayed the start of the removal in response to the pleas of the tribe, and he sought as much medical help for them as possible. But the size of the operation and the greed and venality of many of the contractors chosen to provide supplies to feed and clothe the Cherokees were so enormous as to defeat what little show of humanity was provided. This removal constitutes one of the great tragedies and great crimes ever perpetrated against the Indians by the American people.

Other tribes resisted removal with force. A series of treaties—in particular, the Payne's Landing Treaty of 1832—had been concluded for the removal of the Seminoles in Florida, but the Indians made no effort to leave and Jackson sent them several "talks" (speeches or lectures) to express his displeasure over their tardiness. Many of them were listening to a new tribal leader who had recently emerged, and not their "Great Father" in Washington. This was a mixed-blood chief by the name of Osceola—whites called him Powell—a bold and handsome warrior about thirty-five years of age who fiercely opposed removal and threatened extinction to any Seminole who obeyed Jackson's orders. One chief, Charley Emathla, understood the hopelessness of their situation and was about to leave for the West with a small band of followers when Osceola and his supporters suddenly appeared and demanded an explanation. An argument ensued and Osceola shot Charley Emathla dead and left his body exposed on the trail for all to see. He emptied Charley's pockets and flung the money in every direction.

The militia tried to control the situation, but when a baggage train was seized by Osceola and the soldiers guarding it ambushed, the action triggered the beginning of the Second Seminole War. The date was December 18, 1835. It became a long, bloody, and expensive war. Several American generals were given command to hunt down the Indians in the Florida swamps, but Osceola outfoxed them all—until Major General Thomas S. Jesup arrived. He served for eighteen months and captured and removed nearly 3,000 Seminoles. Then in October, 1837, under a flag of truce, Jesup induced Osceola to meet him to negotiate the release of some captured chiefs. Jesup ordered the meeting place surrounded and when Osceola showed up he was seized and interned at Fort Marion in St. Augustine, where he died a few months later on January 31, 1838. Still the war continued. Not until 1842—six years after Jackson left office—did it end. By that time the government had spent over $15 million on the struggle and suffered the loss of 1,500 regular soldiers. There is no estimate of the mortality among Seminoles or volunteers.

The Creeks also resisted. Jim Henry, "the most redoubtable of the Creek chiefs," led a hopeless effort to turn aside white determination to get rid of them. But the fury of the Indian assault panicked Americans living in Alabama and Georgia. Something like 10,000 troops were sent against the Creeks, and they quickly subdued the Indians. Many of the Creeks were hauled off to the West handcuffed and in chains. Some 14,000 of the tribe were removed during the summer of 1836. They formed a steady stream of starving, sick, frightened, and desperate people. "Our road has been a long one," moaned one old chief. "On it we have laid the bones of our men, women, and children. . . . Tell General Jackson if the white man will let us, we will live in peace and friendship."

In the north the Sac and Fox Indians had been resettled west of the Mississippi but decided to return to their homes in Illinois when they found more difficulties than they anticipated on the great plains. White settlers panicked when the Indians appeared and soon state and federal troops were called in to expel the invaders. Under the leadership of Chief Black Hawk the Indians resisted and fought bravely and well. But this Black Hawk War, as it is known, lasted only a few months. By 1832 the Indians had fled back across the Mississippi River and Chief Black Hawk was taken prisoner.

Black Hawk was imprisoned in Washington for a short time, where he was hauled before President Jackson, and then paraded around the east coast so that Americans could get a good look at a defeated Indian chief. The authorities also wanted to impress upon the Indian the might and almost unlimited resources of the United States to overpower the tribes. Before sending him touring the country, Black Hawk was once again brought before Jackson in Baltimore for a final warning.

The Chief arrived with a small entourage. The "Great Father" stared angrily at him. Then he spoke. "You . . . behaved very badly in raising the tomahawk against the white people, and killing men, women and children upon the frontier. Your conduct compelled me to send my warriors against you, and your people were defeated, with great loss, and your men surrendered, to be kept until I should be satisfied that you would not try to do any more injury." There was a short pause before the President began again. "Your chiefs have pledged themselves for your good conduct, and I have given directions that you should be taken to your own country" after the eastern tour is concluded. "You will see the strength of the white people," Jackson continued. "You will see that our young men are as numerous, as the leaves in the woods. . . . We do not wish to injure you. . . . But if you again plunge your knives into the breasts of our people, I shall send a force, which will severely punish you for your cruelties. Bury the tomahawk and live in peace with the frontiers. . . . And I pray the Great Spirit to give you a smooth path and fair sky to return."

When the President had finished his lecture Chief Black Hawk stepped forward. *"My Father,"* he began, "My ears are open to your words. I am glad to hear them. I am glad to go back to my people. I want to see my family. . . . I ought not to have taken up the tomahawk. But my people have suffered a great deal. When I get back, I will remember your words. I won't go to war again. I will live in peace." Then Black Hawk and the other chiefs withdrew. That evening the chief executive of the United States and an old Chief of the Sac and Fox tribes attended a theatrical performance at the Front Street Theater in Baltimore and both men commanded the attention of the audience. For some in the crowd had never seen an Indian before—or the President of the United States. The two men made a curious and remarkable pair.

Over the next several years all of the Five Civilized Tribes were transported from their homes in the southern states and taken to the Indian Territory which had been established by the Indian Intercourse Act of 1834. But removal did not end here. Northern tribes, like the Sac and Fox Indians, were also expelled from "civilized society." The Chicago Treaty of 1833 with the Chippewa, Ottawa, and Potawatomi tribes provided the United States with valuable land in Michigan, Illinois, Wisconsin, and Iowa. Some ninety odd treaties were signed during the Jackson administration, including those with the Miami, Wyandot, Saginaw, Kickapoo, Shawnee, Osage, Iowa, Delaware, and other tribes. By the close of Jackson's term in office some 45,690 Indians had been removed west of the Mississippi. The United States acquired about 100 million acres of land for about $68 million and 32 million acres of western land.

In insisting upon the removal of the Indian, President Jackson believed that it was the only course of action by the government if the Indian was to be spared certain annihilation. Not that he was motivated principally by his concern for the safety of Native Americans. His main concern was the safety of the United States, and he firmly believed that the Indians constituted a danger and threat to that safety. But he was also convinced that if Indian life and culture were to be preserved then they must remove themselves from the presence of white society.

A twentieth-century historian of the Native Americans, Francis Paul Prucha, has suggested that the American government had little choice in its policy toward the Indians. He believes that there were only four courses of action open: genocide; integration of the two races; military protection of the Indians in their places of residence; removal. No other alternative was possible.

As to the first option there were no doubt some Americans at the time who agreed with Henry Clay when he said in 1825 that the disappearance of the Indian "from the human family will be no great loss to the world," but certainly no one in the Jackson administration ever advocated exterminating Native Americans. That was unthinkable. As for assimilation, neither Indians nor whites favored this option. Most, if not all, whites were racists who regarded Indians as inferior. The possibility of miscegenation outraged and frightened them. Nor did Native Americans want to assimilate. They, too, wished to preserve their unique identity as a people. They had their own laws, religion, constitution, society. Assimilation meant becoming cultural white people, and they totally rejected that prospect. The third option, military protection, was an utter impossibility. Considering the greed and avarice with which Americans hungered for Indian land it would have taken an armed force larger than anything available to the government at the time to keep whites out of Indian territory.

Obviously the first three options were unacceptable. The only remaining option, removal, was the one the administration adopted. And, as Jackson repeatedly said, it was the only policy to pursue if Indian tribes and their culture were to survive. Those tribes that did remove exist today, whereas other tribes in the east disappeared. Still it cannot be denied that removal as implemented by the government proved to be a ghastly price to pay for the survival of Native Americans, one that brought perpetual shame to the nation.

CHAPTER FOUR

Slavery and Union

It is rather fashionable among some historians these days to indict the Democratic party as the party of southern planters intent on defending at all costs their "peculiar institution," slavery. The strong allegiance of the South to Jackson and several of the Presidents who succeeded him, plus the fact that Jackson himself was a slave owner who, at one time, owned 150 slaves, tend to bolster the argument. And not the least of it is the fact that when Martin Van Buren set about structuring a party organization around the Jackson candidacy and wrote to his conservative southern friends, he emphasized the need of party in warding off the attacks of abolitionists. He dismissed the need to create new party feelings. "If the old ones are suppressed," Van Buren told Thomas Ritchie, a leader of the Richmond Junto and editor of the Richmond *Enquirer*, "geographical divisions founded on local interests, or what is worse prejudices between free and slave holding states will inevitably take their place. Party attachment in former times furnished a complete antidote for sectional prejudices by producing counteracting feelings. It was not until that defence had been broken down that the clamour agt Southern Influence and African Slavery could be made effectual in the North."

The Democratic party was not brought into existence to serve the slave-owning needs of one class of the electorate in one section of the country. Van Buren was simply pointing out that where in the past the national interests of southern and northern Republicans were similar, as distinct from those of the Federalists, these interests had been undermined during the one-party era of the Monroe administration. This similarity of interests "can and ought to be revived," he explained to Ritchie, "and the most natural and beneficial to the country is that between the planters of the South and the plain Republicans of the North."

During the ensuing presidential election, Duff Green, editor of the United States *Telegraph* and kinsman of John C. Calhoun of South Carolina, noted that the slavery question had not arisen at all. He was even bold enough to suggest at the end of the 1828 campaign that the "anti slave party in the North is dying away."

It was wishful thinking. The problem of slavery had not yet assumed the overwhelming proportion of importance and danger that it would toward the close of the Jacksonian era. But it was present, however muted, however dodged by worried party organizers. When the admission of Missouri as a slave state had come up for debate in Congress, there was an attempt to end the spread of slavery in the territories that finally concluded with the admission of Missouri as a slave state and Maine as a free state and the exclusion of slavery in the Louisiana Purchase north of 36°30'. The admission of these two states retained the even balance between free and slave states in the nation—and, most important, in the voting of the United States Senate—and thereby resolved one problem in the minds of some politicians. But it meant that Congress had legislated to prohibit the extension of slavery into the territories, a right that would be hotly debated prior to the Civil War. It should not be forgotten, however, that an earlier Congress under the Articles of Confederation passed the Northwest Ordinance of 1787 wherein slavery was prohibited in the territory that later became the states of Ohio, Indiana, Michigan, Illinois, and Wisconsin.

The controversy over slavery during the debates on the admission of Missouri into the Union prompted Thomas Jefferson, living in retirement, to warn that it was just "a speck on our horizon" which might very well "burst on us as a tornado." It deeply alarmed him. It was like hearing "a fire-bell in the night," he said. Indeed the frightening sound of slaves demanding their freedom was heard most shockingly in 1822 when Denmark Vesey, a free mulatto, led a small army of followers—reputedly some 9,000, but that figure was most likely exaggerated by whites—in preparing for a general revolt in Charleston, South Carolina, to escape their servitude. When it was discovered, the retribution was swift and terrible, reflecting the building fear and tension among southern planters. Five companies of South Carolina militia were immediately raised to crush what was seen as a "servile insurrection" to murder all white men in Charleston and rape their women. Hundreds of arrests occurred over the following months and some thirty-five slaves were hanged. Another thirty-seven were banished from the state. With the "conspiracy" crushed, Charleston slave owners breathed a temporary sigh of relief. But they did not forget that the danger of an uprising was ever present and that the blacks might rise up in their fury and indiscriminately massacre whites, just as they had done a short while ago on the island of Santo Domingo in the Caribbean. That dread forever lurked in the southern mind throughout the Jackson era. "Let this never be forgotten," said one man, "that our NEGROES . . . are the *anarchists* and the *domestic enemy*; the *common enemy of civilized society*, and the barbarians who would, IF THEY COULD, become the DESTROYERS *of our race*."

Not ten years later an even worse rebellion occurred. The Nat Turner Rebellion was no doubt the most important slave insurrection in American history. This one virtually knocked the southern planter into a state of permanent fear and terror. Nat Turner was a driven man, some said a religious fanatic. He had a deep faith in his destiny to lead his people to freedom and he was quite prepared to take whatever steps were needed to fulfill that destiny. Unfortunately, it included murder. On August 22, 1831, at a place called Jerusalem in southeast Virginia, Turner, together with nearly a hundred slaves, murdered sixty whites, many of them women and children. As they moved across the countryside the rebels gathered guns, swords, and any other weapon they could find. By the end of the day almost the entire white community had been wiped out. One family was spared because, as Turner explained in his Confession, they "thought no better of themselves than they did of the negroes."

Once the alarm was sounded, the local constabulary rushed to the scene and quickly suppressed the rebellion. It was a bloody massacre. Blacks were slaughtered on the spot, guilty or not. No arrest, no imprisonment, no trial. Instant execution. Some of these bloodthirsty avengers swore that they would kill "every black person they saw in Southampton County." One group of blacks was beheaded. The heads were then hoisted on poles and put out for public display. It is not known how many blacks were executed. No doubt several hundred perished in this mad act of revenge.

The horror of the Turner Rebellion sent shock waves through the South. "Fear was seen in every face," was the opinion of one report. A near-mass hysteria was generated, and it completed the radicalization of many southerners. What added to the fury and tumult was the growing presence of abolitionists, some of whom preached the immediate freeing of the slaves. This movement was undoubtedly rooted in an evangelical Protestant upsurge that was growing more active and vocal at the time. It was advanced by the steady turn toward emancipation that began in New England and moved into New York, New Jersey, and Pennsylvania. By 1846 all the northern states had abolished the "peculiar institution" within their jurisdictions. In view of the fact that Great Britain had declared a general emancipation in the 1830s and that all the South American countries upon gaining their independence freed their slaves, with the exception of Brazil and Cuba, the pressure to end slavery throughout the United States mounted each year during the decades of the 1830s, '40s and '50s.

In 1817 the American Colonization Society was founded for the purpose of returning free blacks to Africa. Its subscribers were mainly southerners who worried about the place of free blacks in their society and wanted to get rid of them by shipping them back "home" to Africa. Over a period of ten years the society probably relocated approximately 1,000 persons to what later became the independent republic of Liberia. Soon important newspapers were founded in the United States to advance the cause of abolition, the first of which was the *Genius of Universal Emancipation*, a Baltimore journal edited by Benjamin Lundy. No doubt the most raucous journalistic voice to be heard on the subject sounded on January 1, 1831, with the appearance of *The Liberator*, edited by William Lloyd Garrison. So violent was his reaction to slavery that Garrison labeled the Constitution "an agreement with hell and a covenant with death"—not a sentiment likely to sit well with either northerners or southerners. He even referred to George Washington as a thief and a kidnapper who "is now in hell!"

The founding of the American Antislavery Society in 1833, the steady increase of antislavery meetings throughout the North, the establishment of a network of stations on an "underground railroad" to assist slaves in their flight to freedom, and the passage by many northern states of "personal liberty laws" which forbade state officials from assisting in the capture and return of fugitive slaves—all added to the building tensions in the nation that threatened the continued existence of the Union.

Worse, race riots became a regular occurrence in Jacksonian America, and the fury of these confrontations resulted frequently in deaths, personal injuries, and the destruction of property. These riots paralyzed the black community with fear because of their savagery. A number of blacks in 1835 were "driven by the violence of an infuriated mob from their homes in Philadelphia" and they took refuge in a small town in New Jersey. Some of these attacks were led by men of "intelligence and wealth," so-called "gentlemen of property." Others seemed provoked by the economic fears of working men. A number of Democratic newspapers tried to reassure southerners that northern workers would never countenance abolition or the blandishments of antislavery agitators. "The working men of the non slave holding States," declared the Washington *Globe*, "have too much intelligence to degrade their condition in life, and diminish the means of comfortable subsistence from the labors of their hands, by encouraging the schemes of abolition societies, which, if successful, would make them competitors for employment with myriads of half-famished blacks."

The rioting even touched the nation's capital. In August 1835, the city of Washington verged on total chaos, "a scene of horrible disorder." What triggered the rioting was the appearance of an abolitionist agent who was caught distributing "incendiary publications among the negroes of the district" which were "calculated to excite them to insurrection and the bloody course" that resulted in the "Nat Turner Rebellion." What maddened the crowd, according to the Secretary of the Navy, was the rumor that President Jackson's mulatto slave, a man named Augustus, was one of the distributors of these "incendiary publications." The rioting went on for days and troops had to be stationed at public buildings, with the windows barricaded. "We could not have believed it possible," lamented the Washington *National Intelligencer.*

A deputation went to the White House and confronted the President. The slave had to go, they told Old Hickory. He must be dismissed from his position. But General Andrew Jackson was not the sort of man to take dictation from the representatives of a mob. He "favored" the deputation with one of his glares of contempt. "My servants are amenable to the law if they offend against the law," he shot back at them, "and if guilty of misconduct which the law does not take cognizance of, they are amenable to *me*. But, I would have all to understand distinctly that they are amenable to me *alone*, and to no one else. They are entitled to protection at my hands, and this they shall receive."

Jackson's position on slavery was the position of many other Democrats in the country, both North and South. It was essentially the one given expression by Representative William O. Goode of Virginia several years earlier. "The right of property exists before society," said Goode. "The Legislature cannot deprive a citizen of his property in his slave. It cannot abolish slavery in a State. It could not delegate to Congress a power greater than its own." Moreover, Democratic leaders argued that the Constitution expressly recognized slavery and made an explicit provision about representation in Congress when counting population in order to accommodate southerners. An agreement had been reached and a contract signed and ratified by which slavery was protected under the nation's constitutional form of government. Congress, therefore, had no power to interfere with it or terminate it. "The existence of slavery is a deplorable evil" and was known to be evil at the time the Constitution was adopted, wrote Harrison Gray Otis, mayor of Boston. But a compact was struck, and "it is our duty and our interest to adhere to it."

"There is no debatable ground left upon the subject," pronounced Jackson's mouthpiece, the Washington *Globe*. Only those who wish to disrupt the Union and jeopardize democracy raise the slavery question, it contended. To Jackson, the abolitionists were wicked and subversive. To achieve their end they would condone violence and bloodshed. They would abrogate the rights of others. Law and order meant nothing to them if it interfered with their determination to bring about emancipation. They claim to be motivated by religion, said Jackson, "the cause of humanity and . . . the right of the human race," but everyone "upon sober reflection, will see that nothing but mischief can come from these improper assaults upon the feelings and rights of others."

To Jackson, abolitionists were troublemakers who hated the democracy because it had displaced their elitist class and they wished to disrupt the Union to regain their lost status and power. Not one of them supported the principles of the Democratic party, he declared. They favored a national bank, public works, and a high, protective tariff—all of which was guaranteed to multiply "the sources of discord with the various sections of the Union." If they are successful in their quest, he later claimed, they will raise upon the ruins of the Constitution "a great consolidated government based upon the combined moneyed power of England and

America, and make the laboring and producing classes of our country, 'hewers of wood and drawers of water' for their own aggrandisement."

Jackson's anger toward abolitionists was not motivated so much by his concern for the preservation of slavery—although as a slave owner himself he undoubtedly reacted in accordance with his own special interests—as for the preservation of the Union. Slavery was guaranteed to disrupt the nation as presently structured under the Constitution. Such a disruption, he feared, would ultimately cost "oceans of blood & hundreds of millions of money to quench" and in the process halt the advance of democracy.

The danger of sectional discord had already raised its frightful head in the Missouri controversy. And there was no way to tell in advance whether a simple incident or seemingly insignificant issue raised in Congress might touch off an explosion that would shake the Union. One came very close to doing just that at the tail end of Jackson's first administration. On the surface it did not appear that slavery was involved in any way—and indeed slavery did not trigger the near-calamity that followed. But in the minds of some Americans, slavery was the ever-present concern, lurking, waiting to devour the nation in controversy and possible bloodshed.

What triggered the dispute was a quarrel over the tariff. And this disagreement soon broadened into a question involving the right of a state to nullify federal law and even secede from the Union if its grievances were not redressed. It moved the nation close to civil war.

Since the War of 1812 and the development of northern manufactures there was a steady and rising demand for protective tariffs to safeguard home industries from foreign competition. The first protective tariff was passed in 1816. Not much later southerners began to express their resentment over protection because they found that increasingly they must sell their cotton in an open, worldwide market but buy needed manufactures on a closed market protected by federal law. A law that discriminated in favor of one section of the country at the expense of another was patently unfair, according to these critics. Consequently, when the Democratic leaders in Congress decided to raise tariff rates just prior to the presidential election of 1828 in order to oblige those states whose electoral support Jackson needed most, they touched a raw southern nerve. Several southern Congressmen swore they were tricked into believing a higher tariff would be defeated. Instead, the rates were jacked up so high in 1828 that the package was called a "Tariff of Abominations." During the presidential campaign Jackson himself stated that he favored a "judicious" tariff—whatever that meant—and Henry Clay laughed at the ambiguity of the remark by declaring that he favored an "*in*judicious" tariff.

John C. Calhoun, the Vice President, returned home after the passage of the Tariff of Abominations to write an "Exposition and Protest" in condemnation of the tariff, which the South Carolina legislature adopted without revealing the name of the author. Calhoun's protest was directed at a government that used its power to pass legislation detrimental to one part of its constituency. Here was an instance, he said, in which the majority shoved its collective will down the throats of the minority—in this case the slave-owning South. And what could be done? What machinery existed by which the minority could protect itself against the tyranny of the majority? What power did it have?

In his paper of protest Calhoun tried to provide an answer. He advanced the doctrine of nullification, which argued that when the federal government acted in conflict with the interests of a particular state, that state could declare such action void within its borders; in other words, nullify the legislation. If three-fourths of all the states also nullified the offending legislation, then the law was repealed, just as if the Constitution itself had been amended. This doctrine of "interposition," according to Calhoun, would protect minority rights and prevent any tyranny by the majority. For liberty could best be protected by denying the central government absolute authority to advance its will. By maintaining strong states, he declared, the cause of liberty and the rights of all men would be secured. But if, after applying the doctrine of interposition, the nullifying state was coerced by the federal government, then the state had the right to secede from the Union. However, secession was meant as the last resort. The doctrine of nullification was intended to prevent secession, said Calhoun.

These radical views got a thorough airing in Congress early in its first session after Jackson's inauguration. In January 1830, Senators Daniel Webster of Massachusetts and Robert Y. Hayne of South Carolina hotly debated Calhoun's theory and with it the nature of the Union. The debate erupted suddenly by a seemingly innocent resolution restricting the further sale of public lands until those already on the market were sold. But straightaway the argument shifted to the rivalry between sections and then to the problem of slavery.

In a thoughtful and powerful speech Hayne defended slavery, states rights, and the doctrine of nullification. The Union could only be maintained, he said, if the rights of the South were respected and protected. That included slavery. The protection of slavery under the Constitution had brought the states into a federated Union and any violation of that protection would necessitate action by the state to safeguard its interests. The national government was the mere agent of the states, he contended, its powers being derived from the authority of the sovereign states. Only the states are sovereign, and their sovereignty is indivisible. The Union was nothing more than a compact of states.

It was a remarkably effective speech. Its arguments had a logic that seemed incontrovertible, given its premise about the nature of the Union; and its exposition of the historical record proved far more authentic than anything Hayne's critics could present. But Daniel Webster felt equal to the task of rebuttal and in a two-day effort he laid waste (in the minds of many northerners) the notion that the Union was merely a confederation of states. It was a Union of people, he declared. "I go for the Constitution as it is, and for the Union as it is," he thundered. "It is, Sir, the people's Constitution, the people's government, made for the people, made by the people, and answerable to the people." It was the argument Jackson himself would adopt, the basis of his contention that the nation had become a democracy.

Webster closed his second reply to Hayne in a noble statement that can still stir emotions about the grandeur and wonder of liberty provided by the American system of government. But it also warned of the dire consequences should the people fail to preserve it.

While the Union lasts, we have high, exciting, gratifying prospects spread out before us, for us and our children. Beyond that I seek not to penetrate the veil. God grant that in my day, at least, that curtain may not rise! God grant that on my vision never may be opened what lies behind! When my eyes shall be turned to behold for the last time the sun in heaven, may I not see him shining on the broken and dishonored fragments of a once glorious Union; on States, dissevered, discordant, belligerent; on a land rent with civil feuds, or drenched, it may be, in fraternal blood! Let their last feeble and lingering glance rather behold the gorgeous ensign of the republic, now known and honored throughout the earth, still full high advanced, its arms and trophies streaming in their original lustre, not a stripe erased or polluted nor a single star obscured, bearing for its motto no such miserable interrogatory as "What is all this worth?" nor those other words of delusion and folly, "Liberty first and Union afterwards"; but everywhere, spread all over in characters of living light, blazing on all its ample folds, as they float over the sea and over the land, and on every wind under the whole heavens, that other sentiment, dear to every true American heart—Liberty and Union, now and forever, one and inseparable!

Liberty *and* Union! They were inextricably joined, said Webster. Without Union there is no liberty. The death of one guaranteed the annihilation of the other.

These ideas perfectly matched those of Andrew Jackson. He hated the idea of nullification, and secession was an abomination in his mind. As President, he felt he must express his opinion in a clear and forceful manner. He must let the country know what he thought about this "most pernicious doctrine."

His opportunity came on April 13, 1830, when Democrats in Congress held their regular commemorative celebration to honor the birth of Thomas Jefferson. Fearful that the "nullies" would use the occasion to recruit additional supporters, Jackson felt he must scotch the effort with a bold declaration of his personal commitment. He considered a number of possibilities. He consulted with his closest advisers and together they decided on his appropriate course of action.

The dinner was held at the Indian Queen Hotel. Toasts were invited. Jackson rose to provide the first, and according to tradition he supposedly looked directly at John C. Calhoun as he spoke.

"Our Union," he cried: *"It must be preserved."*

Utter silence. His meaning was thunderously clear. Senator Hayne later asked Jackson to amend his statement to include the word "federal" so that his toast might be printed as "Our *Federal* Union: *It must be preserved."* This had been Jackson's original version of the toast as shown to his advisers so he did not hesitate to allow the amendment.

Vice President Calhoun followed with his toast. "The Union," he declared: "Next to our liberty, the most dear; may we all remember that it can only be preserved by respecting the rights of the States and distributing equally the benefit and burden of the Union."

Calhoun went on too long. He should have stopped after the word "dear." No matter. His meaning was perfectly obvious. In his mind liberty was the sole consideration, and only the support of the states could insure its preservation.

Among the many dangers Jackson was trying to prevent by his toast was the possibility of the "nullies" capturing the states-rights position. Those who believed in nullification and secession would—and eventually did—give states rights a bad name. They would succeed in making states rights virtually synonymous with secession and the breakup of the Union.

The ties that had once bound Jackson and Calhoun were permanently severed by the end of Old Hickory's first administration. There were many reasons, not the least of which was their conflicting interpretation of the nature of the Union. And what started as a verbal disagreement soon boiled over into something more serious. When Congress passed the Tariff of 1832 and removed some of the "abominations" of the 1828 law, it modified but did not lower tariff rates to any significant degree. In effect, the new tariff remained at a relatively high level. Still it was an improvement, however modest. Unfortunately, it was not acceptable to the southern hot-heads, who seemed intent on total surrender when it came to protection. For some this single issue summed up all their fears and apprehension about slavery, states rights, and the liberty to pursue a distinctive southern way of life.

At one time Calhoun was restrained in his radicalism by a hope that he would succeed Jackson to the presidency. But that was now gone. He was unacceptable to the Old Hero, who chose instead his now constant adviser, Martin Van Buren. Egged on no doubt by his frustrations and disappointments, Calhoun urged the governor of South Carolina, James Hamilton, Jr., to apply the doctrine of nullification to the new tariff and declare it inoperable within the state. The federal government, he said, had no authority to coerce a state into obeying a law it regarded as a violation of its rights.

Governor Hamilton responded to the rising sense of outrage within South Carolina by calling a special session of the state legislature, which in turn ordered an elected convention to meet on November 19, 1832, to take appropriate action. As expected, since the "nullies" were organized throughout the state, they controlled the convention and on November 24, 1832, passed an Ordinance of Nullification by a vote of 136 to 26. The Ordinance declared the tariff laws of 1828 and 1832 "null, void, and no law, nor binding" upon South Carolina, its officers or citizens. After February 1, 1833, it would be unlawful to collect the payment of duties. It warned the federal government against any attempt to coerce the state into compliance. Should force be used, the state would secede and "forthwith proceed to organize a separate Government."

Jackson responded immediately. He issued a Proclamation dated December 10, 1832, in which he spoke directly to the people of South Carolina and warned them of the consequences if they proceeded to carry out the threat of the Ordinance. But he took care not to sound unyielding or unduly menacing. He tried to sound forgiving and understanding to the people of his native state, but at the same time he wanted them to realize that he would never tolerate defiance of federal law. He had his duty prescribed by his oath of office. He had no alternative but to enforce the laws of the land. "Those who told you that you might peacefully prevent their execution deceived you. . . . Their object is disunion. But be not deceived by names. Disunion by armed force is *treason*. Are you really ready to incur its guilt? If you are, on the heads of the instigators of the act be the dreadful consequences; on their heads be the dishonor, but on yours may fall the punishment. On your unhappy State will inevitably fall all the evils of the conflict you force upon the Government of your country."

More important than the impassioned rhetoric of the Proclamation was its systematic refutation of the doctrine of nullification and secession. "I consider, then," said Jackson, "the power to annul a law of the United States, assumed by one State, *incompatible with the existence of the Union. . . .*" The people of the United States formed the Union, he went on, not the states. "We are *one people* in the choice of President and Vice President." His renewed claim that the chief executive represented all the people and was responsible to them culminated Jackson's efforts to redefine the relationship between the electorate and the President.

The Constitution "forms a *government*," he declared, "not a league." A single nation was formed to which the states surrendered "essential parts of sovereignty" in "becoming parts of a nation." The federal government, not the states, declares war, makes treaties, and coins money. The states are not sovereign, he continued. The people are the sovereign power. Their will is absolute. And the Union is perpetual.

The Proclamation comes close, says a modern historian, "to being the definitive statement of the case for perpetuity" of the Union. Abraham Lincoln drew most of his arguments against secession from the Proclamation. And the Supreme Court in 1869 could find no additional arguments supporting the case for perpetuity than those contained in Jackson's statement. It was a great state paper for which the President could thank Edward Livingston, his Secretary of State at the time, for its constitutional arguments.

Jackson's statement is far greater than Webster's more celebrated "second reply." Webster offered sentiment and a heartfelt appeal for the preservation of the Union; Jackson provided a dynamic and modern new reading of the nation's constitutional structure.

As might be expected, the Proclamation failed to find favorable comment in South Carolina. It was greeted with "scorn & contempt as the mad ravings of a drivelling dotard."

Old Hickory did not rely on his Proclamation alone. At the same time he warned South Carolinians against illegal action he also began to prepare for the possibility of civil strife. He alerted the naval forces in Norfolk to prepare a squadron to proceed to Charleston if called upon; he notified the fort commanders in South Carolina to gird themselves for possible attack, and military equipment was rushed to Fort Pinckney; and he directed several thousand troops to the Carolina border—all under the command of General Winfield Scott. Jackson also contacted Unionists within South Carolina. He regularly corresponded with Joel R. Poinsett, former minister to Mexico. "I repeat to the union men again," he wrote, "fear not, *the union will be preserved* and treason and rebellion put down, when and where it may shew its monster head."

To demonstrate what he meant Jackson told Van Buren that he would go to Congress in order "to cloath our officers and marshall" with the necessary authority to enforce the law. This must be done before February 1, he said, the cutoff date for the collection of tariff duties in South Carolina. On January 16, 1833, he formally sent his Force Bill message to Congress, in which he asked for authorization to deploy the military to put down armed rebellion. Although the Washington *Globe* called it a "collection bill," many southerners called it a "bloody bill" and a "war bill."

When the Unionists in South Carolina heard Jackson's reassurance that he would stand strong against "treason and rebellion" they wept with joy. *"Enough,"* they cried. "What have we to fear, we are right and God and Old Hickory are with us."

In the meantime Calhoun resigned as Vice President—the first to do so—and got himself elected to the U.S. Senate, where he could continue the fight at the center of the gathering storm. Hayne, whom he replaced, returned home and was elected governor. As the danger of secession and war escalated, the efforts of many statesmen were directed toward preventing a confrontation that could produce violence. What finally resulted was the Compromise Tariff of 1833, which Henry Clay shepherded through Congress and which Calhoun pronounced acceptable to the nullifiers. This new tariff would provide a ten-year truce in which rates would slowly fall, taking a sharper drop in the final years of the truce, when the duties would stand at a uniform 20 percent *ad valorem* and remain at that rate. Both the Force Bill and Compromise Tariff were passed at approximately the same time, and Jackson signed them on March 2, 1833.

A convention was subsequently reconvened in South Carolina and the state declared its satisfaction with the Compromise Tariff by repealing its Ordinance of Nullification. But in a show of defiance the convention nullified the Force Bill. "If this be no more than a swaggering conclusion of a blustering drama," sniffed the Washington *Globe*, "it will speedily be consigned to the contempt of an enlightened and patriotic public."

"Nullification is dead," Jackson rightly concluded. But the danger inherent in the controversy still lingered on. "The next pretext," he warned, "will be the negro, or slavery question."

Indeed. The Democratic party may not have come into being to safeguard the institution of slavery, but it had no intention of doing anything about it. The flaws in the Constitution that had been deliberately put there would remain. As far as Democrats were concerned, the situation of the black man had been permanently decided in 1787. Any effort to change the agreement, in their minds, was doomed to failure and certain to disrupt the Union. They wanted a static situation even though every sign warned that the status quo could not continue. They chose to close their eyes and close their ears. And Jackson's fearful prediction came true.

RICHARD III.

Top: In Natchez, a part of New Spain in 1789, Jackson took an oath of loyalty to the King of Spain. The third page of the oath, which contains Jackson's signature, is shown here.
Source: Archivo General de Indias, Seville, Spain
Middle: Jackson in full military uniform as a major general of the Tennessee Militia, painted by his friend and companion, Ralph E. W. Earl, c. 1815.
Source: Courtesy of the National Portrait Gallery
Bottom: A caricature of Jackson as the notorious King Richard III of England, 1836.
Source: Collection of The New York Historical Society

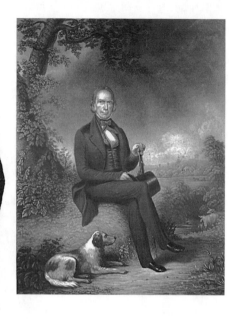

Top Left: In the presidential election of 1828, the National Republicans published a "Coffin Handbill" listing the names of the American militiamen who were executed during the Creek War. The Democrats responded with their "Coffin Handbill," reproduced here, reminding Americans of the great military victory in 1815.
Source: Courtesy of the Tennessee State Museum

Opposite top right: A painting of Henry Clay, looking statesmanlike, and seated in his garden at Ashland in Lexington, Kentucky, c. 1843.
Source: Courtesy of the National Portrait Gallery
Opposite bottom: This is a daguerrotype of Martin Van Buren taken late in life, c. 1856.
Source: Courtesy of the National Portrait Gallery

Right: A sour and rather dyspeptic looking portrait of John Quincy Adams executed c. 1844.
Source: Courtesy of the National Portrait Gallery
Bottom: A large crowd like the one shown here descended on the White House following Jackson's inauguration on March 4, 1829.
Source: Library of Congress

Left: The distinguished orator and statesman, Daniel Webster, who ran only once for the presidency in 1836, but tried many times after that to secure a nomination from his party. Portrait , 1846.
Source: Courtesy of the National Portrait Gallery
Bottom: Political cartooning came of age during the presidential election of 1832 between Jackson and Clay. This one concerns the public credit which the National Republicans, and later the Whigs, accused Jackson and the Democrats of ruining.
Source: Courtesy of the Boston Public Library, Print Department
Opposite Top: The notorious "Trail of Tears" along which the Cherokees were forced to march to their new residence in the Indian Territory.
Source: Woolaroc Museum, Bartlesville, Oklahoma

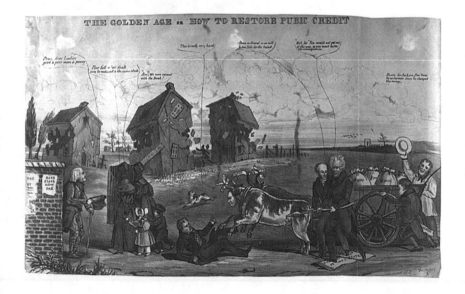

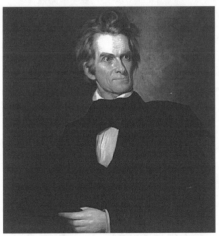

Above: Something of the intensity of John C. Calhoun's physical appearance and intellectual power is caught in this painting, c. 1845.
Source: Courtesy of the National Portrait Gallery
Right: The great Chief Black Hawk of the Sac and Fox tribe who tried to recover his nation's lands in Illinois in the Black Hawk War, but was defeated by a superior force. Taken prisoner, he was paraded through eastern states before being permitted to return to his tribe.
Source: Library of Congress, #14836 26

TIPPECANOE AND TYLER TOO.

What has caused this great commotion, motion, motion,
 Our country through?
 —It is the ball a-rolling on,

CHORUS.
For Tippecanoe and Tyler too—Tippecanoe and Tyler too,
 And with them we'll beat little Van, Van;
 Van is a used up man;
 And with them we'll beat little Van.

Like the rushing of mighty waters, waters, waters,
 On it will go,
 And in its course will clear the way,
  For Tippecanoe and Tyler too, &c.

See the Loco standard tottering, tottering, tottering,
 Down it must go,
 And in its place we'll rear the flag
  Of Tippecanoe and Tyler too, &c.

Have you heard from old Kentuck, tuck, tuck,
 Good news and true?
 Seventeen thousand is the tune,
  For Tippecanoe and Tyler too, &c.

Have you heard from old Varmount, mount, mount,
 All honest and true—
 The Green Mountain boys are rolling the ball,
  For Tippecanoe and Tyler too, &c.

Don't you hear from every quarter, quarter, quarter,
 Good news and true?
 That swift the ball is rolling on,
  For Tippecanoe and Tyler too, &c.

The New York boys turned out in thousands, thousands, thousands,
 Not long ago—
 And at Utica they set their seals
  To Tippecanoe and Tyler too, &c.

Now you hear the Van-Jacks talking, talking, talking,
 Things look quite blue—
 For all the world seems turning round,
  For Tippecanoe and Tyler too, &c.

Let them talk about hard cider, cider, cider,
 And Log Cabins too—
 'Twill only help to speed the ball,
  For Tippecanoe and Tyler too, &c.

The latch-string hangs outside the door, door, door,
 And is never pulled through—
 For it never was the custom of

CHORUS.
Old Tippecanoe and Tyler too—Tippecanoe and Tyler too,
 And with them we'll beat little Van, Van;
 Van is a used up man;
 And with them we'll beat little Van.

He always has his tables set, set, set,
 For all honest and true—
 And invites them in to take a bite,
  With Tippecanoe and Tyler too, &c.

See the spoilsmen and leg treasurers, treasurers, treasurers,
 All in a stew—
 For well they know they stand no chance,
  With Tippecanoe and Tyler too, &c.

Little Matty's days are number'd, number'd, number'd,
 Out he must go—
 And in the chair we'll place the good
  Old Tippecanoe and Tyler too, &c.

Now who shall we have for our governor, governor, governor?
 Who! tell me who?
 Let's have Bill Seward, for he's a team
  For Tippecanoe and Tyler too, &c.

O have you heard the news from Maine, Maine, Maine,
 All honest and true?
 One thousand for Kent, and seven thousand gain,
  For Tippecanoe and Tyler too, &c.

O have you heard from Georgia, Georgia, Georgia,
 Good news and true?
 That brave old State will go they say,
  For Tippecanoe and Tyler too, &c.

Have you heard from Maryland, land, land,
 News that makes little Van blue?
 They've shown they won't vote for a *used up man*,
  But for Tippecanoe and Tyler, too, &c.

The beautiful girls, God bless their souls, souls, souls.
 The country through—
 Will all to a *man* do all that they can,
  For Tippecanoe and Tyler too, &c.

Above: The rollicking lyrics to "Tippecanoe and Tyler Too" sung during the Log Cabin Campaign in 1840 when William Henry Harrison, the hero of the battle of Tippecanoe Creek, and his running mate, John Tyler, defeated Martin Van Buren and Richard M. Johnson.

Opposite top left: James Knox Polk, known as Young Hickory, was a "dark horse" presidential candidate of the Democratic Party in the presidential election of 1844, but he defeated the Whig candidate, Henry Clay. Daguerrotype, c. 1846.
Source: Courtesy of the National Portrait Gallery

The Rats leaving a Falling House.

Top Right: This cartoon depicts the collapse of Jackson's first cabinet, when all the members resigned, except the Postmaster General. Each "rat" is identified by face.
Source: Collection of The New-York Historical Society
Bottom: Ralph Waldo Emerson, undoubtedly the most influential intellectual of the middle period of American history. Lithograph, 1881.
Source: Courtesy of the National Portrait Gallery

Left: Thomas Hart Benton, who fought Jackson in a gunfight in Nashville, but later became his political ally in the United States Senate. He served in the Upper House for thirty years. Portrait c. 1861.
Source: Courtesy of the National Portrait Gallery
Bottom: A political cartoon (1844) lampooning the Democrats.
Source: Collection of The New-York Historical Society

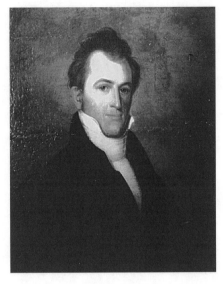

Right: Andrew Jackson Donelson, Jackson's ward and secretary, whose wife, Emily Donelson, served as the First Lady during Jackson's administration.
Source: Courtesy The Hermitage
Bottom: General Zachary Taylor's extra-ordinary victory over the Mexicans at Palo Alto during the Mexican War catapulted him to a presidential nomination in 1848.
Source: Library of Congress, #LC-USZ62 -19243

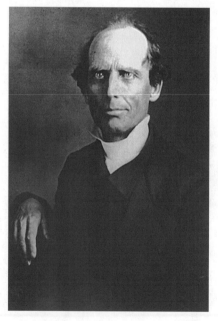

Top: The Prophet, Joseph Smith, founder of the Church of the Latter-Day Saints, was assassinated in Carthage, Illinois. Brigham Young succeeded Smith and led the Mormons across the Plains to the Great Salt Lake where they established Deseret.
Source: Courtesy of the National Portrait Gallery

Bottom: Charles Grandison Finney, the most influential of the evangelical Protestants who undoubtedly originated modern revivalism in America.
Source: Courtesy of the Oberlin College Archives, Oberlin, Ohio

Opposite Top: The United Society of Believers in Christ's Second Appearance, otherwise known as "Shakers" because of their distnctive ritual, shown here doing a wheel-within-a-wheel dance.
Source: Leslie's Popular Monthly

Opposite Bottom: A typical camp meeting in which believers hoped to purge their souls of sin and obtain the peace and assurance of salvation.
Source: Library of Congress

Top: Andrew Jackson's study at The Hermitage, which connected to his bedroom. The Ladies' Hermitage Society, who has charge of his home, has successfully furnished the room exactly as Jackson knew it. Bottom Right: Rachel Jackson, the beloved wife of the seventh President, who died of a heart attack shortly after her husband was elected President in 1828. Bottom Left: Hannah, the faithful servant of the Jacksons, who was with Rachel at the moment of her mistress's death. Source: All courtesy of The Hermitage: Home of President Andrew Jackson.

CHAPTER FIVE

The Reach for Perfection

Probably the most important development during the Jacksonian era was the powerful urge to reform and improve society and the conditions developing from an increasingly industrial and materialistic nation. "The demon of reform"—to use Ralph Waldo Emerson's phrase—had been loosed in the land and no one escaped it. Some of the efforts were feeble and insignificant. Others, like abolitionism, rocked the nation. All added to the texture, excitement, and wonder of American society in the Age of Jackson.

The American of the early nineteenth century was a hustler, a man on the make, invariably alert to any opportunity which might improve his station in life. Money meant everything. "No man in America is contented to be poor, or expects to continue so," remarked one foreign traveler. "Go ahead." "Get ahead." That was the spirit of the Jacksonian age. "The whole continent presents a scene of *scrambling* and roars with greedy hurry," was the comment of one visitor. "Go ahead! is the order of the day." It is "the real motto of the country." "Our age," agreed Senator Daniel Webster, "is full of excitement" and rapid change.

It was a materialistic society Americans were building, one dedicated to business, trade, and the acquisition of wealth. Once in place it became permanent—the creed to which most Americans in future generations subscribed. The doctrine of the "self-made man," that is, "rags to riches," became the gospel of America. The term "self-made man" was invented in the Jacksonian era, and Andrew Jackson himself was its personification. Americans did not expect "greatness" to be thrust upon them—although they would have assuredly accepted it under any circumstances. They knew and believed that they had to work for their success. "Work," lectured one man, "and at eighteen you shall . . . live in plenty, be well clothed, well housed, and able to save." All good things necessarily followed. "Be attentive to your work, be sober and religious, and you will find a devoted and submissive wife; you will have a more comfortable home than many of the higher classes in Europe." This Puritan work ethic had been prevalent in America since the arrival of the first English settlers, but it now took on a special urgency and new purpose. "He who is an active and useful member of society," declared one, "who contributes his share to augment the national wealth and increase the numbers of the population, he only is looked upon with respect and favor."

Because they were so economically motivated, Americans at the beginning of the nineteenth century were able to develop an extraordinarily successful economy, one which grew rapidly during the first few decades of the century and eventually raised the United States to the highest economic level. The Industrial Revolution arrived shortly after the War of 1812; manufactures developed; capital expanded; and a transportation revolution began with the feverish building of roads, bridges, and canals. Steamboats started plying the great rivers, and the building of the Baltimore and Ohio Railroad inaugurated the start of the railroad era in transportation. This Market Revolution tripled the number of banks operating in the country and sent the amount of money in circulation soaring from $20 million to over $60 million. Throughout Jackson's term in office the economy ballooned. The nation had reached the "take off" stage in becoming an industrial society. Only the Panic of 1837 caused a momentary setback. It was a sharp rebuke to a seemingly unstoppable prosperity. But within a few years the economy was off and running again.

In explaining this phenomenal development, an English commission sent to America in 1851 to discover the reasons for this economic success reported: "The extent to which the people of the United States have as yet succeeded in manufactures may be attributed to indomitable energy and an educated intelligence, as also to the ready welcome accorded to the skilled workmen of Europe."

Not only "skilled workmen" but also farmers and laborers were migrating to America in increasing numbers, and they spread out to both cities and rural areas just as the United States was expanding across a continent. In less than fifty years, aided by the acquisition of Texas in 1845 and the acquisition of California, Arizona, New Mexico, and Utah following the Mexican War, a nation that had once been a small collection of British colonies huddled along the Atlantic coastline exploded across a continent. The highways, turnpikes, canals, and railroads built during the first half of the nineteenth century provided arteries to send a constant flow of people and commodities from city to town to remote communities all over the nation, binding them together and pumping economic life into them. Cincinnati, Chicago, St. Louis sprang up virtually overnight, while older cities like New York, Boston, Philadelphia expanded at a rapid pace. "What a country God has given us!" cried Jackson in a moment of spontaneous enthusiasm. "How thankful we ought to be that God has given us such a country to live in."

Much of the enthusiasm and faith in America was based on the fact that the intellectual currency of the Jacksonian era was minted in the Enlightenment and embossed in a Romantic age. Americans were the product of an age which preached the perfectibility of man, the inevitability of improvement, and the supremacy of reason in all things. They believed in their own ability to improve their condition in life and to participate in the reform and advancement of society. There was in America a rising tendency, said William Ellery Channing, a New England clergyman, to exalt the people based on a "devotion to the progress of the whole human race."

Although Americans were zealous about improving their economic condition in life—"I know of no country, indeed," wrote Alexis de Tocqueville, in his classic work, *Democracy in America,* "where the love of money has taken stronger hold of the affections of men" than in the United States—nevertheless, they were also intent on improving social conditions generally. They were committed, continued Tocqueville, to the philosophical theory "that man is endowed with an indefinite faculty for improvement." This comes in large measure from American belief in equality, he said. Aristocratic nations tend to narrow the scope of human perfectability, he continued, while democratic nations, like the United States, expand it virtually beyond reason. As an example of what he meant, Tocqueville cited an incident in which he asked a sailor why American ships were built to last only a short time. "The art of navigation," replied the sailor, "is every day making such rapid progress that the finest vessel would become almost useless if it lasted beyond a few years."

Improvement! Human perfectability! Americans worked constantly toward improving ships, tools, machines, institutions, whatever, in order to bring about "the indefinite perfectability of man." In social terms that meant reform. And reform meant the need to revitalize and humanize social institutions, to improve the conditions in which men and women work and live, and to seek the good of one's fellow man—these were some of the important objectives of these extraordinary Americans of the Jacksonian age. Reformers were intent on raising "the life of man by putting it in harmony with his idea of the Beautiful and the Just."

By the 1820s this romantic impulse had begun to sweep across the United States. Although the old commitment to the ideas of the Enlightenment, such as the efficacy of reason and order, continued to persist, the new age emphasized the sensate in man. Reason alone no longer ruled as the sole perceiver of truth and beauty. Now the emotions were granted a prominent role. Human feelings were no longer suspect; they could now be enjoyed and appreciated. Man's intuitive powers were reckoned a mighty instrument in the search for knowledge and truth and self-improvement. "One day," wrote Emerson, "all men will be lovers; and every calamity will be dissolved in the universal sunshine."

The most obvious expression of the romantic age was the Transcendental movement. This New England creation went beyond a belief in man's goodness by proclaiming man's divinity. Transcendentalists—and they included such men and women as George Ripley, Bronson Alcott, Orestes Brownson, Margaret Fuller, Ralph Waldo Emerson, Henry Thoreau, and many others—believed that the world comprised an infinite variety of different beings, all united in the spiritual power of God which Emerson, the greatest exemplar of Transcendentalism, called the over-soul. The over-soul was diffused in man and nature, and man through intuitive contemplation could hear the voice of the Almighty. Actually, Transcendentalists were mystics in their approach to knowledge, for they believed that man could "transcend" experience and reason to discover through his intuitive powers the mysteries of the universe. "Pantheism is said to sink man and nature in God," wrote one Transcendentalist; "Materialism to sink God and man in nature; and Transcendentalism to sink God and nature in man."

A number of Transcendentalists met regularly in the home of George Ripley, a Boston minister. Emerson attended after returning from a tour of Europe, where he encountered the influence of such British writers as Coleridge and Wordsworth, as well as the German philosopher Immanuel Kant. He settled in Concord, Massachusetts, where he turned out an endless stream of poems and essays, all espousing the ideas and concepts of the Transcendental movement. Like others in the movement, Emerson reacted strongly against the corrupting influence of the new industrial society of his age. In his famous essay "Man the Reformer" he wrote: "What is man born for but to be a Reformer, a Re-Maker of what man has made, a renouncer of lies; a restorer of truth and good, imitating that great Nature which embosoms us all?" He was widely read in his own day, especially after he took to the lecture circuit, where his discourses profoundly impressed a large mass of people.

After Emerson, Henry Thoreau was the most noteworthy Transcendentalist. He attended Harvard, taught school briefly, and then settled at Walden Pond, where he spent two years (1845–1847) in virtual isolation. His masterpiece, *Walden*, is a superbly written account of his experiment in living close to nature. It contains his philosophic, religious, and economic views, many of them highly critical of accepted opinions and beliefs. "I went to the woods because I wished to live deliberately, to front only the essential facts of life, and to see if I could learn what it had to teach, and not, when I came to die, discover that I had not lived." He recognized, as he said, that "the mass of men lead lives of quiet desperation." That was not for him. Thoreau urged men to value their freedom and simplify their lives. He challenged them to aspire to greatness. "I learned this, at least, by my experiment: that if one advances confidently in the direction of his dreams, and endeavors to live the life which he has imagined, he will meet with a success unexpected in common hours. . . . He will live with the license of a higher order of beings."

Because he believed the Mexican War was immoral, Thoreau refused to pay a Massachusetts tax and preferred to be jailed rather than allow a sovereign state to coerce his free will. He wrote his vastly important "Civil Disobedience," a work that greatly influenced Mahatma Gandhi and Dr. Martin Luther King. "If a plant," said Thoreau, "cannot live according to its nature, it dies; and so a man."

Transcendentalists saw beauty in nature but ugliness everywhere else, especially in the nation's social institutions. The materialism of the day was particularly disturbing, and in many ways Transcendentalism can best be understood as essentially a revolt against materialism. Its disciples denounced society's concern for things. Theodore Parker, a New England minister, used his pulpit to scorch the conscience of a genteel society grown preoccupied with money and material gain. Quite obviously, he was a dangerous agitator and troublemaker in the minds of some of his parishioners.

Many of the Transcendentalists had been raised with a strict religious background. They were ministers or the children of ministers. And what is significant is that many of the reforms of the Jacksonian era were led by religious leaders who believed with a holy zeal in the justice and urgency of what they preached. Some of them felt they pursued a divine mission. They had a calling. But that was a notion that permeated the thinking of many Americans as they banded together in organizations to reform society and ameliorate the human condition. Among any number of important and worthwhile things, they set out to improve penal institutions and insane asylums, end slavery, provide equal rights for women, promote temperance, help the poor and distressed, better working conditions, and foster peace around the world.

Religion, then, provided an important source of creative energy for the reform movements that raked the countryside during the Jacksonian age. Where Transcendentalism was confined pretty much to the New England area, the religious impulse of the early nineteenth century, the so-called Second Great Awakening, affected Americans around the country and provided much of the intellectual and spiritual power of many of the reforms that developed during this era.

Muted at first, and then dismissed later on, were the Puritan beliefs in a stern deity, alert to all infractions of divine law. The notion of sin-prone man hounded by a wrathful God was discarded during the Second Great Awakening. "There is an infinite worthiness in man," declared Emerson, that enables him to surmount all obstacles hindering his advance in wisdom and goodness. Man's *likeness* to God—the touch of divinity that separated and distinguished him from the lower orders—was emphasized; man was not so much depraved (as the result of Adam's fall) as deprived. God's love embraced all and forgave all.

The notion that God would save everyone was a basic precept of the Universalist Church whose teachings were brought to this country in 1779 by John Murray (1741–1815) and became popular during the Jacksonian era. Universalist circuit riders spread the faith westward to the frontier and it became one of the largest Protestant denominations prior to the Civil War. Its powerful message of equality appealed to all, especially its assurance that if equality was not achieved in this life it would surely come in the next.

In religious terms the Second Great Awakening emphasized the ability of each person to achieve salvation through submission to the lordship of Christ. The freedom of the will and the right intention of the individual were all important in working out one's salvation. The notion of an elect chosen by God had not the same force and urgency in the individualistic age of Jackson as it had during the colonial period. Anyone could obtain salvation and at any time once they heard God's call and responded. The notion of a theocratic aristocracy was swept aside, just as Jackson's political revolution had swept aside the political aristocracy. The democratic spirit of the age blew powerfully through the Christian churches and brought with it thousands seeking religion and the saving comfort of divine love. They crowded into revival or camp meetings to purge their souls of sin and seek the peace and assurance of salvation. Once saved through conversion, repentance and a firm commitment to reform, it then became their duty to save others. This constituted the very core of the evangelist movement of the first half of the nineteenth century. Evangelists carried their missionary zeal to all sections of the country, finding their most receptive audiences in the west and south.

Evangelists emphasized the belief that God could and did choose anyone, even the most unlikely, to preach His message. Traditional ordination was unnecessary, indeed a hindrance. Priests, ministers, bishops, a theology degree from Harvard or Yale—all were deemed unessential in this new democratic surge. Anyone could speak directly to God, receive His message, and then preach it to the masses. Because evangelists emphasized the role of the individual they most influenced those religious denominations that were the least ritualistic, namely the Congregational, Methodist, Baptist, and Presbyterian churches. When an educated eastern cleric arrived in St. Louis prepared to take up his ministry he was greeted with derision. An article in a religious newspaper sneered at him, stating that he had come to draw a salary and dictate religious belief. "The preaching manufactories of the east," snorted the paper, "appear to be engaged in sending hirelings to the west, and should any of those man-made, devil-sent, place-hunting gentry come into our country, and read in our places, we shall likely rise up against them, and send them packing."

The preaching of revivalists had little content except what was drawn directly from the Bible. Whereas the old theocratic elite defined a congregation's theology, evangelists urged their followers to think for themselves and decide for themselves what was and was not morally permissible. The Declaration of Christian Association of Washington, Pennsylvania, an independent religious society, declared: "We are persuaded that it is high time for us not only to think, but also to act for ourselves; to see with our own eyes, and to take all our measures directly and immediately from the Divine Standard." Like Jackson, evangelists preached that the people could be trusted to do what was right.

Charles Grandison Finney (1792–1875) was the most prominent evangelist of the day and undoubtedly the originator of modern revivalism in America. Born in Connecticut he moved to New York where he studied law. After an extraordinary religious experience in 1821 he abandoned the law to argue "the case for God" and began preaching in western New York. Like many another "self-made man" of his day he rose from relative obscurity to become the most prominent minister in the country. As a traveling evangelist he journeyed across the so-called "burned-over district" of western New York along the route of the Erie Canal, leaving audiences mesmerized by the power of his preaching. He hated the clerical hierarchy; and he hated the theological "hairsplitting" so typical of "eastern seminaries." Like Jacksonian politicians, Finney patterned his style after the new democratic model. "What do politicians do?" he asked. "They get up meetings, circulate handbills and pamphlets, blaze away in the newspapers, send their ships about the street on wheels with flags and sailors, send coaches all over town, with handbills, to bring people up to the polls, all to gain attention to their cause and elect their candidate." Well, we do the same thing. "The object of our measures is to gain attention and you must have something new."

To attract crowds he and other evangelists engaged in practices that horrified established churches. Their camp meetings quickly evolved into emotional debauches with wild scenes of men and women confessing their sins, weeping, and tearing their hair in a desperate display of repentance. Some in the congregation even got down on their hands and knees and barked at trees where they presumed they had trapped the devil. And virtually everyone at the camp grounds responded to the preaching with shouts of "Amen! Amen! Jesus! Jesus! Glory! Glory!" They applauded, booed, and whistled to register their approval or disapproval and they voted with their feet by "shopping around" for preachers who pleased them, a practice that became standard in American religious life.

Frances Trollope, who lived for several seasons in the United States and wrote a book on *The Domestic Manners of Americans*, attended a camp meeting in Indiana in 1829 because she had heard that the experience "was like standing at the gate of heaven, and seeing it opening before you." She had also heard that "it was like finding yourself within the gates of hell." She therefore decided to see for herself and was so shaken by what took place around her that she retreated in panic and disbelief.

At midnight a horn sounded to summon the crowd of 2,000 from private to public worship, reported Trollope. A preacher took his place by a stand and began to speak in a low nasal tone. He told the crowd that "this was the time fixed upon for anxious sinners to wrestle with the Lord," that he and his brethren were there to help them. He urged those who needed help to come forward into "the pen," which was a space immediately below the preacher's stand.

The crowd fell back at the mention of the pen and other preachers came down from their stand and walked among the crowd and starting singing hymns. Soon a hundred or more men and women came forward "uttering howlings and groans, so terrible," related Trollope, "that I shall never cease to shudder when I recall them." At the command, "let us pray," the assembled mass "fell to its knees; but this posture was soon changed for others that permitted greater scope for the convulsive movements of their limbs; and they were soon all lying on the ground in an indescribable confusion of heads and legs." The "hysterical sobbings, convulsive groans, shrieks, and screams the most appalling burst forth on all sides." One very pretty girl started tearing her hair. "Woe! Woe to the backsliders!" she screamed. "Hear it, hear it Jesus! When I was fifteen my mother died, and I backslided, oh Jesus, I backslided! Take me home to my mother, Jesus! Take me home to her, for I am weary!" Another cried out: "I will hold fast to Jesus, I never will let him go; if they take me to hell, I will still hold fast, fast, fast." And this emotional orgy, said Trollope, went on all night.

At daybreak the horn sounded again and within an hour the whole camp was "joyously and eagerly employed in preparing and devouring their . . . breakfasts as if the night had been passed in dancing." The shrieking and howling had ended, and the pale pretty faces, so "demoniac" the night before, stood "simpering beside a swain," carefully serving him coffee and eggs.

Finney preached that those who had been born again and acknowledged Christ's lordship and sovereignty over them should "aim at being holy, and not rest satisfied till they are as perfect as god." They must look beyond themselves. "The evils have been exhibited," he cried, "the call has been made for reform. . . . Away with the idea that Christians can remain neutral and keep still, and yet enjoy the approbation and blessing of God. It is part of Christian duty," to aid the ignorant, the destitute, and the unfortunate. "It becomes Christians to imitate their Master, and to seek the good of those who are careless of their own good."

Finney's approach to religion blended so perfectly with the spirit of the Jacksonian age that he and his many imitators enjoyed enormous success and ultimately shaped the standard form of evangelical Protestantism as practiced to this day. Theodore Dwight Weld (1803–95) experienced a conversion under Finney and trained seventy itinerant preachers—"a Holy Band"—to bring God's saving message to the masses. In addition to his revivalist crusade Weld himself became a potent advocate for temperance and abolition.

Small wonder, then, that the "demon of reform" took hold. Americans saw the evils in society and, galvanized with religious fervor, felt they could expel them through concerted, organized action. They understood their duty and acted upon it. The acceptance of the idea of the perfectibility of man brought suggestions and schemes to hasten the perfecting process and clear away the obstacles that blocked it. Men and women organized themselves around one or another of these schemes and held meetings, gave speeches, raised money, and issued printed propaganda to advance their cause. Some hyperactive souls joined several different reform movements at once, such as abolition, temperance, women's rights, and even sabbatarianism, the movement to enforce the strict observance of Sunday, including the shutting down of post offices. These reformers were volunteers in an army to scourge the nation of the social blight that disfigured it.

Education was a needed target for reform. In the past proper schooling was often limited to those whose parents could afford the expense; those less fortunate spent the rest of their lives hobbled by this disadvantage. James Parton, Jackson's first biographer, declared that Old Hickory was so ignorant of law, history, politics, science, "of everything which he who governs a country ought to know," that he was imprisoned in a cage of ignorance against which he periodically raged like a wild beast.

Henry Clay was another poorly educated statesman who relied, he said, on his "genius" to get ahead in the world. One contemporary claimed that if he had had the education Jefferson and Madison enjoyed he would have been a greater statesman than either of those two men.

On the other hand Daniel Webster graduated from Dartmouth College. His father sacrificed everything he had to give his son a proper education. As a child Webster remembered that his father once pointed to a man who was a congressman. "My son," said the father, "that is a worthy man, he is a member of Congress . . . he gets six dollars a day, while I toil here. It is because he had an education, which I never did. If I had had his early education, I should have been in Philadelphia in his place. . . . I could not give your elder brothers the advantages of knowledge, but I can do something for you. Exert yourself, improve your opportunities, learn, learn, and when I am gone, you will not need to go through the hardships which I have undergone, and which have made me an old man before my time." Webster became the most celebrated lawyer and orator of his day. Moreover, he earned the equivalent of what to-day would be millions of dollars through his law practice.

Education slowly but steadily improved during the Jacksonian era. The number of American colleges virtually doubled. At the same time free primary education was winning acceptance in this increasingly democratic society, and in 1821 Boston established the first public secondary school. Not much later Massachusetts required all towns with a population in excess of 500 families to provide free secondary schooling. The rest of the country was not nearly as progressive, but it was a start, and the idea slowly advanced across the country during the next several decades.

In the forefront of those advocating free public education was Horace Mann, the most significant figure in American education during the Jacksonian period. He, along with others, argued that free education meant the eventual elimination of poverty and the general prosperity of the entire nation. He said it would reduce crime, improve social justice, and strengthen the nation's institutions. "Health, freedom, wisdom, virtue, time, eternity," cry out in behalf of education, he said. "Some causes have reference to temporal interests; some to eternal;—education embraces both." As secretary of the Massachusetts Board of Education, he fought for and won higher appropriations from the legislature, with which he built better schools, improved the curriculum, obtained a minimum six-month school year, and won higher salaries for teachers. He also established the first teacher-training (normal) school in Lexington, Massachusetts, to prepare teachers for their vocation. Because of his concern for their future lives, that they have meaning and purpose, Mann shared a truth with a graduating class at Antioch College in Ohio just a few weeks before his death: "Be ashamed to die until you have won some victory for humanity."

Women's colleges did not begin until after the Civil War, but due to the efforts of such women as Emma Willard and Mary Lyon, institutions of learning for women at the secondary level were improved. Willard founded the Female Seminary in Troy, New York, and Lyon opened Mount Holyoke Seminary in South

Hadley, Massachusetts. In 1833 Oberlin College in Ohio inaugurated co-educational instruction by admitting women and African Americans for the first time. On the question of the education of women, Catherine Beecher, who founded a number of seminaries for women, said:

It is to *mothers*, and to *teachers*, that the world is to look for the character which is to be enstamped on each succeeding generation, for it is to them that the great business of education is almost exclusively committed. And will it not appear by examination that neither mothers nor teachers have ever been properly educated for their profession. What is *the profession* of a *Woman*? Is it not to form immortal minds, and to watch, to nurse, and to rear the bodily system, so fearfully and wonderfully made, and upon the order and regulation of which, the health and well-being of the mind so greatly depends?"

The improvement in public education for all the citizens of the various states and communities around the country also stimulated the improvement of textbooks. The earliest manuals were generally poor in quality, and not until Noah Webster introduced his *Spelling Book* and *Reader* did it materially improve. In 1836 William H. McGuffey's *Eclectic Reader* appeared and had a tremendous impact on elementary school instruction. The Reader emphasized cultural and moral standards and preached a patriotism that inculcated a devotion to country that satisfied the growing sense of nationalism that had been building since the War of 1812. Unquestionably, McGuffey had a greater impact on the shaping of American morality than any writer or politician of the period.

Of particular educational significance during the 1830s was the lyceum movement, a program of public lectures on the arts and sciences. The movement began in Great Britain and was introduced into this country by Josiah Holbrook, who founded the first lyceum in Massachusetts in 1826. Soon the system spread across the northern states and several thousand lyceum organizations were in operation by the 1840s. Famous statesmen, scientists, clergymen, and educators spoke to audiences on a wide range of subjects, from religion and science to art, music, and literature. Ralph Waldo Emerson, Oliver Wendell Holmes, and Daniel Webster were a few of the very popular speakers who lectured around the country.

The advancement of science in the educational process was less rapid than it should have been. This may have been caused in large measure by the preference of most Americans for applied scientific techniques over pure scientific theory. In turn this can be explained by the pragmatic cast of the American mind. "Where in Europe young men write poems or novels," commented one foreign observer, "in America, especially Massachusetts and Connecticut, they invent machines and tools." Indeed, a number of important machines and tools were invented during the Jacksonian era, including the mechanical reaper for harvesting grain, invented by Cyrus H. McCormick in 1831; the revolver by Samuel Colt in 1835; the process of vulcanizing rubber by Charles Goodyear in 1839; the telegraph by Samuel F. Morse in 1844; the sewing machine by Elias Howe in 1846, and many others.

Despite the seeming preference for technology by Americans, the United States was not without individuals of stature in science. At Harvard University the geologist and zoologist Louis Agassiz was a most popular teacher and lecturer who emphasized original research and profoundly influenced a generation of scientists. Asa Gray, a botanist at Harvard, made important contributions to his field and helped popularize the study of botany. At Yale, Benjamin Silliman taught chemistry and founded and edited the *American Journal of Science and Arts*. Elizabeth Blackwell graduated first in her class at medical school and went on to establish the New York Infirmary for Women and Children which founded one of the first cancer clinics in the country and still operates today. But perhaps few individuals of this period made as great a contribution to science as John James Audubon, whose magnificent drawings in *Birds of America* became justifiably popular and remain so.

One of the most important discoveries in the entire history of medicine occurred during the Jacksonian age. A dentist by the name of William T. G. Morton discovered anaesthesia in 1842, a discovery also claimed by at least three other men. It can be imagined what the practice of medicine was like before anaesthesia. For example, President Jackson had a bullet removed from his upper left arm in 1832 in a "simple" surgical procedure performed in the White House without any anaesthesia whatsoever. Nineteen years earlier he had been shot by Jesse Benton, the brother of Senator Thomas Hart Benton of Missouri, in a gunfight, and the bullet had not been removed because Jackson feared losing his arm. By 1832, the bullet had worked itself to the inner side of his arm and less than an inch from the surface of the skin. It also began to cause him a good deal of pain. So the sixty-four-year-old Jackson summoned Dr. Harris of Philadelphia to the White House to remove the bullet. The procedure was swift. Jackson bared his arm, gritted his teeth, grasped his walking stick, and said, "go ahead." The surgeon made an incision with a scalpel, squeezed the arm, and out popped a "half ball" of the ordinary pistol size. The wound was bandaged and Jackson went right back to his presidential work. Once anaesthesia was discovered surgical operations around the world became more complicated and frequent, saving many lives in the process.

An educated and literate citizenry gave promise of the development of a national literature. And a veritable galaxy of distinguished writers emerged during the Jacksonian era. One such notable writer was Washington Irving who wrote on a variety of American subjects. Although his *Rip Van Winkle* and *Legend of Sleepy Hollow* stories drew from European folktales he set them in the Catskill Mountains of New York. Another outstanding author was James Fenimore Cooper. His *Leatherstocking Tales* glamorized Indian and frontier life and captured the beauty of the American forest. He described with compelling force the conflict of cultures between Indians and whites. *The Pioneers* (1823), *The Last of the Mohicans* (1826), and *The Deerslayer* (1841) marked a shift away from the formal, classical lines of the Enlightenment to the new romanticism of the Jacksonian era, providing readers with excellent portraits of life on the frontier.

Still a third distinguished writer, who was a critic of Transcendentalists and rather pessimistic about man and his future, was Nathaniel Hawthorne. His novels remain current because of their extraordinary psychological insights into the efforts of men and women to overcome sin and guilt. Born in Salem, Massachusetts, in 1804, he lived in Concord, where he met the advocates and experienced the ideas of the new Transcendental movement. His reputation was established with the publication of *Twice-Told Tales* in 1837, a collection of stories which depicted the struggles of guilt-ridden men and women. In his greatest novels, *The Scarlet Letter* (1850) and *The House of Seven Gables* (1851), the human situations of his characters are grim and terrible.

A writer of greater power and stylistic skill was Herman Melville. He, too, was imbued with the mystery and terror of sin. Born in New York in 1819, he went to sea without finishing his education. He deserted ship in the South Seas and lived among cannibals, later making his way to Tahiti, where he became a beachcomber for a short time. Returning home, he wrote out his adventures in two books: *Typee* (1846) and *Omoo* (1847). In his extraordinarily powerful novel *Moby Dick* (1851), Melville grappled with the problem of man's unending struggle with evil. Ahab, the captain of a whaling ship, spends his life pursuing a white whale which personifies all that is wicked and beautiful, dangerous and compelling in life. The majesty of the language and the philosophic depth of its content place it in the highest class of literary masterworks. At one point in *Moby Dick,* Melville paid tribute to Andrew Jackson and the democracy that bore his name. The language is also heavily saturated with Transcendental thought and feeling:

Men may seem detestable . . . but man, in the ideal, is so noble and so sparkling . . . that over any ignominious blemish in him all his fellows should run to throw their costliest robes. . . . But this August dignity I treat of, is not the dignity of kings and robes, but that abounding dignity which has no robed investiture. Thou shall see it shining in the arm that wields a pick or drives a spike; that democratic dignity which, on all hands, radiates without end from God; Himself! The great God absolute! The centre and circumference of all democracy! His omnipresence, our divine equality!

If, then, to meanest mariners, and renegades and castaways, I shall hereafter ascribe highqualities, though dark; weave round them tragic

graces; . . . if I shall touch that workman's arm with some ethereal light
… then against all mortal critics bear me out in it, thou just Spirit of
Equality, which hast spread one royal mantle of humanity over all my
kind! Bear me out in it, thou great democratic God! . . . Thou who didst
pick up Andrew Jackson from the pebbles; who didst hurl him upon a
warhorse; who didst thunder him higher than a throne! Thou who, in all
Thy mighty earthly marchings, ever cullest Thy selectest champions from
the kingly commons; bear me out in it, O God.

Another outstanding writer of this period, but one who more
nearly represents the romantic movement rather than Transcendentalism, was Edgar Allan Poe. Raised in the South, he spent
most of his life in New York and Philadelphia writing mysteries,
poetry, and short stories, some of which are singularly inventive
and fresh. Many credit him with inventing the detective story with
Murders in the Rue Morgue and *The Purloined Letter.* He was one
of the first to write what is called science fiction and showed extraordinary mastery of horror stories with such works as *The Pit
and the Pendulum* and the *Cask of Amontillado.* The French were
the first to recognize his genius, and they saw him as an artist
whose unearthly visions brought on by drink went unappreciated
by his own countrymen. Poe's poems *The Raven, The Bells,* and
Annabel Lee, along with such stories as *The Gold Bug, The Mask
of the Red Death,* and *Fall of the House of Usher,* brought him
considerable attention, if not fame.

Several poets of this age won distinction, sometimes because
they too condemned aspects of their society and preached reform.
The most outstanding poets of the period included Henry Wadsworth
Longfellow, James Russell Lowell, and John Greenleaf Whittier.
Lowell satirized the Mexican War in his *Bigelow Papers,* while
Whittier served the cause of abolitionism by attacking slavery in his
poems. Longfellow was the most popular poet of all, although future gen-
erations found his works less original than did his contemporaries.

But the real poetic genius of the antebellum age was Walt
Whitman, whose *Leaves of Grass* is one of the landmarks of American literature. He was born on Long Island in New York in 1819 and
trained as a journalist. He held a succession of jobs and even

taught school and worked as a carpenter. His poetry restated the Transcendental themes of man's goodness and the beauty and wonder of nature. An ardent Jacksonian, he believed passionately in democracy, and his writings sing of its worth. "I never before so realized the majesty and reality of the American people *en masse*," he wrote after watching troops march home from war. "It fell upon me like a great awe."

> One's self I sing, a simple separate person,
> Yet utter the word Democratic, the word En-Masse.

Whitman's poetry was uniquely American and the forms he used were original and inspired. True recognition of his genius did not come, however, until after his death in 1891.

Another literary talent whose genius was not recognized until after her death was Emily Dickinson. This shy, reclusive child of Amherst, Massachusetts once wrote

> I'm nobody! Who are you?
> Are you—Nobody too?

At an early age she read Emerson and soon thereafter began writing verse. When she died she left more than seventeen hundred poems, only seven of which were published in her lifetime, and they were little noticed. But she had a sense of her worth. "I have a horror of death," she wrote; "the dead are soon forgotten. But when I die they'll have to remember me." And they have. Between 1890 and 1945 her poems were slowly brought to light and published. In many of her poems she confronts the questions of who she is and what her relationship is to other people. Her poetic techniques were ahead of the times but each word she chose expressed deep emotion and personal conviction. She is unquestionably one of the finest American poets, certainly the finest woman poet, in U.S. history.

Although the South did not produce literary figures during this period to match those of New England and New York, still there were several writers who produced books of more than common interest and value. William Gilmore Simms wrote a number of romantic novels about the Old South, including *The Yemassee* (1835) and *The Partisan* (1835). Augustus B. Longstreet, who wrote *Georgia Scenes* (1835), and Joseph Baldwin, who penned *The Flush Times of Alabama and Mississippi* (1853), tried to capture the rawness and vitality of backwoods life. But as Simms himself said, "The South don't give a d—n for literature or art." And certainly not for authentic American literature which described the life of the southerner's surroundings.

The development of a national literature also brought the improvement and increase in the number of newspapers and magazines. In 1810 there were 350 newspapers in the United States, as opposed to forty at the conclusion of the American Revolution. When Andrew Jackson was elected President in 1828, it was estimated that the number had risen to 600, of which fifty were dailies, 150 semiweeklies, and the remainder weeklies. The rise of the "penny press," an inexpensive and highly effective instrument to reach a large and growing audience, had a powerful impact in shaping the attitudes and behavior of masses of Americans. The first thing that strikes a stranger to America, wrote one touring Englishman, is the extraordinary number of newspapers. "They meet him at every turn, of all sizes, shapes, characters, prices, and appellations. On board the steamer and on the rail, in the counting-house and the hotel, in the street and in the private dwelling, in the crowded thoroughfare and the remotest rural district, he is ever sure of finding the newspaper. There are . . . papers purely political, others of a literary cast, and others again simply professional; whilst there are many of no particular character, combining everything in their columns." Some of the more distinguished newspapers included the New York *Evening Post,* the Washington *National Intelligencer,* and the Richmond *Enquirer.* During the Jacksonian era the New York *Tribune* and *Times* were added to the list of outstanding journals.

But a new style of journalism appeared in the Jacksonian era called the penny press, naturally enough, because each newspaper cost only a penny. Benjamin Day of New York's *The Sun* inaugurated it. He captured a mass circulation among the city's working classes by providing lurid accounts of American life, usually taken from police blotters, instead of the customary political news and mercantile reports. When a revivalist preacher by the name of Matthias was tried for murder the penny press found the perfect vehicle for its style of journalism. The trial had everything the new genre desired: religion, weird social behavior, "licentiousness and lust," sexual depravity, murder, and fraud. While the rest of America focused their attention on such great issues as slavery, nullification, and the destruction of the national bank when reading their newspapers, New York readers reveled in the Matthias affair. Day's *The Sun* soon attracted imitators. It set the standard for future newspapers.

Of magazines there were approximately forty notable publications at the start of the nineteenth century; these tripled by the close of the Jacksonian age. Among the most distinguished examples of magazines founded during the period were the *North American Review, Godey's Lady's Book,* the *Southern Literary Messenger,* and *The Dial,* an organ of New England intellectuals and writers. Later, in the 1850s, *Harper's New Monthly Magazine* and *The Atlantic Monthly* were established.

Since wisdom as well as beauty could be found in nature, the romantics of this age, especially the Transcendentalists, urged everyone to establish a close and real relationship to it. Painters in the Jacksonian era picked up on this interest in nature and produced magnificent landscapes of some of the most impressive scenic wonders in America. The Hudson River school of landscape painting, as it was called, produced many fine works depicting the Hudson River valley, and it included such excellent artists as Thomas Cole, George Inness, and Asher Brown Durant.

In sculpture America was less prodigious. Hiram Powers, whose Greek Slave won him acclaim far beyond the worth of the piece, and Horatio Greenough, whose statue of George Washington was placed on the grounds of the Capitol, were probably the most outstanding artists of this underrepresented genre.

In architecture one of the most distinctive early figures was Charles Bulfinch, who developed the so-called federal style that became very popular and persisted well into the 1820s. The federal style was somewhat Georgian in appearance, reflecting Bulfinch's regard for English form. But it was no mere imitation. It was graceful and elegant, without ostentation, and included such typical touches as the oval parlor, spiraling staircases, smooth facades, and ellipse-topped doorways. Bulfinch rebuilt Faneuil Hall; produced Colonnade Row, whose nineteen joined facades fronted the Boston Common; designed capitols in Augusta (Maine), Hartford, and Boston, and directed the completion of the national Capitol. Many of the leading political figures of the Jacksonian era lived in federal-styled homes.

Another outstanding architect of this period was Thomas Jefferson. Eschewing the British and colonial forms, Jefferson found in the architecture of antiquity the models he felt were best suited to this country. In time, city halls, banks, capitols, and other public buildings were constructed in this style. Not only Roman forms but French houses impressed Jefferson, for it was at his request that a Frenchman by the name of Pierre C. L'Enfant was engaged to plan the capital city on the Potomac River. Jefferson's designs were used for the building of the University of Virginia and the capitol at Richmond; but perhaps his best-known work was his own house at Monticello, a structure on which he worked for nearly forty years.

The forms of antiquity eventually replaced the federal style in the Jacksonian era. They were advanced and developed by such artists as Benjamin Henry Latrobe, William Strickland, and Robert Mills. More and more they tended to emphasize the Greek rather than the Roman form, and they even erected Egyptian obelisks. Strickland designed the Second Bank of the United States building on Chestnut Street in Philadelphia, from which site Nicholas Biddle ran its operations. The building is a near-perfect replica of a Greek temple. Mills designed the United States Treasury building, with its majestic colonnade, and erected a monument to George Washington in Baltimore which was a simple Doric column with a statue of Washington standing on top.

But the man most responsible for the Greek revival in the United States was Benjamin Latrobe. He designed the Capitol in Washington, the Bank of Philadelphia and, along with James Hoban, was responsible for building the White House. President Jackson himself added the north portico to the White House, which Latrobe designed, that gives the mansion its distinctive and impressive outward appearance. It was the feeling of these architects that Greece, in both its democracy and its art forms, provided the best models for adoption in a new, republican land. However, toward the end of the Jacksonian period a new architectural form began to crowd out those of the Greek and Roman. Gothic architecture became the popular design. Its high turrets, arches, and buttresses gave a house a massive look that people with wealth found to their liking. Perhaps the best-known structure of this type is the parent building of the Smithsonian Institution in Washington, the so-called Castle on the Mall, designed in 1846, and appropriately serving as the "nation's attic."

The artisans, mechanics, and workmen who built these imposing structures were also the objects of reformers, for the improvement of labor and working conditions in the cities had long been advocated by social critics. "No man can be a Christian," wrote the Transcendentalist Orestes Brownson, "who does not refrain from practices by which the rich grow richer and the poor poorer, and who does not do all in his power to elevate the laboring classes . . . so that each man shall be free and independent." By the late 1820s there appeared a Workingmen's party and the beginning of a trade union movement. Abolition of imprisonment for debt, free public education, mechanics lien laws, higher wages, and a ten-hour workday were some of labor's demands. Such labor leaders as George Henry Evans, Thomas Skidmore, Seth Luther, and Ely Moore tried to stir the conscience of the nation about the problems of urban workers, and many of their demands were subsequently met. Some of these leaders gave the union movement a genuine radical cast because of their attacks upon private property, one unique in the history of the American labor movement. Crime exists in society, wrote one labor leader, not because of the "natural depravity of man" but because of the "unequal distribution of wealth." "Give to every man a competency," he declared, "and nine-tenths of the poverty and crime now existing would disappear."

One criticism often heard against the formation of unions was the fear that they would set a "dangerous precedent." Ely Moore, a printer and first president of the General Trades' Union of New York, agreed. "It may, indeed, be dangerous to aristocracy, dangerous to monopoly, dangerous to oppression, but not to the general good or the public tranquility."

Through the use of strikes and political agitation the unions made notable progress in the 1830s, but they sustained a near-fatal blow when the Panic of 1837 plunged the nation into a long and harrowing depression. In a notable ruling in the case *Commonwealth* v. *Hunt* in 1842, Justice Lemuel Shaw of the Massachusetts high court declared that trade unions and strikes were legal. Also significant in labor history was President Van Buren's order that no one was to work more than ten hours a day on federal public works, an order that was written into the laws of a half dozen states over the following fifteen years.

Because of increased urbanization and the social blight that frequently accompanies it on account of poverty, political corruption, and indifference to those in need, the delinquency of children grew to alarming proportions. Many of these children were runaways or simply abandoned by their parents and left to their own devices to beg and steal in order to survive. The problem attracted the worthy efforts of reformers who founded houses of refuge for these children in such cities as new York, Philadelphia, and Boston. But life was hard and discipline strict in these "reform schools" and it took many years before those who studied juvenile delinquence recognized that these children were mostly victims, not criminals.

Other victims attracted needed help. Prostitutes in the large cities who wished to reform their lives and escape their unhappy lot could not do it on their own, and many sincere ministers and their congregations raised funds and established houses of refuge for them.

One of the most remarkable and most successful reformers of the Jacksonian period was Dorothea L. Dix, who spent the greater portion of her life working to win improvements in mental institutions, called insane asylums at the time. She tried to help the unfortunate souls inhabiting the asylums by reading portions of the Bible to them each week. But the conditions she observed shocked and angered her. After investigating conditions in Massachusetts she gathered an impressive array of facts and presented them in 1843 in a *Memorial to the Legislature of Massachusetts.* "I proceed, gentlemen," she wrote, "briefly to call your attention to the *present* state of insane persons confined within this Commonwealth, in *cages, closets, cellars, stalls, pens! Chained, naked, beaten with rods,* and *lashed* into obedience." Her documentation embarrassed Massachusetts into building a new institution. For the next fifteen years she extended her work into other sections of the country, winning reform and correction in numerous states and contributing to the building of nearly two dozen new mental hospitals.

A similar movement produced a demand for the reform of prisons. Alexis de Tocqueville, who toured the United States in the 1830s to study American prisons for the French government, commented on this movement. "A few years ago some pious people undertook to make the state of the prisons better. The public was roused by their exhortations, and the reform of criminals became a popular cause. New prisons were then built. For the first time the idea of reforming offenders as well as punishing them penetrated into the prisons." Although the old prisons remained as monuments to the barbarities of the Middle Ages, he noted, the new ones were durable tributes to the gentleness and enlightenment of the modern age. They reflected the Jacksonian belief that man was perfectible, that he could be reformed, and that to a very considerable degree he could control himself and the world around him.

Since so many of the "pious people" who initiated these reforms were women, and since the condition of women had deteriorated badly since colonial days, it was no wonder that they began an agitation for women's rights. Industrialization and urban growth gradually changed gender roles over the past several decades because men were absent from the home during the day, earning a living in a business establishment or factory, while women were forced to remain at home to care for the children and keep the house clean, do the wash, and prepare the meals. Men no longer shared household chores that had been common during the previous century. Such chores were now regarded as "women's work." A "cult of domesticity" evolved by which the ideal woman was characterized as domestic, religious, subordinate, obedient, and mild mannered, the moral guardian of the home. As Lucy Stone told a woman's rights convention in 1855, "I was disappointed when I came to seek a profession." Every employment was closed "except those of the teacher, the seamstress, and the housekeeper." Disappointment, she said, was woman's lot in marriage, in education, in religion, "in everything." She vowed to devote her life to deepening "this disappointment in every woman's heart until she bows down to it no longer." She was joined in her efforts by such indomitable women as Frances Wright, Lucretia Mott, Susan B. Anthony, and Elizabeth Cady Stanton who militantly lectured and agitated for the rights of their sex.

"We believe," read one memorial on women's rights, "the whole theory of the Common Law in relation to woman is unjust and degrading, tending to reduce her to a level with the slave, depriving her of political existence, and forming a positive exception to the great doctrine of equality as set forth in the Declaration of Independence." So these feminists held a convention at Seneca Falls, New York, in 1848, in the Wesleyan Methodist Church, a revivalist church recently formed to agitate for abolitionism, where they issued a Declaration of Sentiments which was patterned after the Declaration of Independence. "When, in the course of human events," read the Declaration, "it becomes necessary for one portion of the family of man to assume among the people of the earth a position different from that which they have hitherto occupied, but one to which the laws of nature and of nature's God entitle them, a decent respect to the opinions of mankind requires that they should declare the causes that impel them to such a course. We hold these truths to be self evident, that all men and women are created equal. . . ." They called for sexual equality and the extension of the suffrage to include women. Although they did not succeed in widening the franchise beyond providing a good beginning to that long-term struggle, they did help to improve the status of women, particularly in their right to control their own property. For example, in 1860, New York gave women the right to sue in court and to control their earnings and property.

Women were among the most persistent reformers when it came to temperance. The formation in Boston of the American Temperance Union in 1826 was the beginning of a crusade that probably will never end. The movement not only attracted women, but many men, particularly clergymen. The idea of the crusade was to get people to sign the "cold water pledge" to give up alcohol. Once given to Demon Rum, argued temperance propaganda, a man soon descends into the depths. "He is now a drunkard, his property is wasted, his parents have died of broken hearts, his wife is pale and emaciated, his children ragged, and squalid, and ignorant. . . . He is useless, and worse then useless; he is a pest to all around him." By 1833 a national organization existed to bring about universal abstinence. The crusade gained momentum with the organization of the Washington Temperance Society in Baltimore in 1840 by half a dozen reformed alcoholics. Since it was generally believed by many prohibitionists that most crimes were the product of liquor abuse, there was a demand that the state exercise its privilege of legislating what some people could not control. Under the leadership of Neal Dow, the movement won its earliest success in Maine, where the first prohibition law was passed in 1846. This was supplanted in 1851 by a statewide law forbidding the sale and manufacture of intoxicating liquor. Other states followed this example until the 18th amendment establishing nationwide prohibition was enacted early in the twentieth century. After fourteen years this amendment was repealed, however, early in the administration of President Franklin D. Roosevelt.

A particularly interesting, if less successful, reform movement of the Jacksonian era was one dedicated to peace. Agreeing with Quakers that war was one of the most terrible and frightening of man's institutions, these reformers sought to establish societies to propagate the necessity of international arbitration and the abolition of war. William Ladd of New Hampshire was the principal architect of the American Peace Society, founded in 1828 in New York City. Later he devised a scheme for the establishment of a court and congress of nations where controversies could be amicably resolved. Another important leader was Elihu Burritt, who organized a number of peace conferences in Europe and wrote extensively on the need to "dethrone the sanguinary monster, War." Nations must learn to abhor the beast. "Working men of the United States!" he exclaimed. "Voters of a young republic! what example will you set at the polls to the hard-working myriads of your brethren in the Old World who lack your right of suffrage to dethrone the sanguinary monster, War! Shall your great officers of the nation be 'peace, and your exactors, righteousness?' or shall 'garments roll in blood,' and fiendish feats of human butchery, qualify your candidate for the highest honour within a nation's gift?" Unfortunately, the Mexican War and the agitation of slavery that eventually led to the Civil War frustrated the efforts of the peace reformers. Not until the twentieth century and the shedding of blood by millions did the movement receive the respect and attention it rightfully deserved.

American law also developed a distinctly American cast during this period, evolving as a kind of reform of the English law that had been basic to the legal system during the colonial period. American law tended to codify into constitutional forms and written codes much of what Britain enjoyed as part of its long tradition. Because of the dearth of judges, American law relied more on juries, and the jury system found favor in a country devoted to democratic forms. This helped to make courts more popular than they had been in the colonial era. As a consequence, lawyers became a political upper class and the most influential group in their communities.

Andrew Jackson was both a lawyer and a judge. In 1798, at the age of thirty-one, he was elected by the Tennessee legislature to a seat on the bench of the state superior court, often called the supreme court because its judges sitting together comprised Tennessee's highest tribunal. He wore a judicial gown in court and tradition reports that he maintained the dignity and authority of the bench and that his decisions were unlearned but generally correct. On one occasion while Jackson was holding court in a little village, a great, hulking fellow named Russell Bean, who had been indicted for cutting off the ears of his infant child in a "drunken frolic," sauntered into court, cursed the judge and jury, and then marched out the door. "Sheriff," Judge Jackson called out in his most judicial voice, "arrest that man for contempt of court and confine him."

The sheriff immediately proceeded after Bean but soon returned empty-handed. The culprit refused to return to court. "Summon a posse, then," the judge commanded. So off the sheriff went accompanied by a posse, but again he returned without his prisoner. Bean had immobilized the posse by threatening to shoot the "first skunk that came within ten feet of him."

Jackson almost turned purple with rage. "Summon me," he shouted at the sheriff. "Well, judge, if you say so," responded the sheriff. At that Jackson adjourned the court for ten minutes and bolted out the door. He found Bean a short distance away, in the center of a crowd, cursing and flourishing his weapons and promising instant death to anyone who attempted to arrest him.

Mr. Justice Jackson walked straight up to Bean, a pistol in each hand. "Now," he roared, staring into the eyes of the culprit, "surrender, you infernal villain, this very instant, or I'll blow you through."

Bean looked into Jackson's blazing eyes and saw something terrible. Then he meekly surrendered. A few days later, while sitting in jail, he was asked why he gave in so readily to Jackson after defying an entire posse. "Why," he replied, "when he came up, I looked him in the eye and I saw shoot, and there wasn't shoot in nary other eye in the crowd; and so I says to myself, says I, hoss, it's about time to sing small, and so I did."

Andrew Jackson made a very effective backwoods judge. There was "shoot" in his eyes, and sane men did not trifle with that.

One of the most intriguing and significant efforts to carry reform into the daily lives of ordinary people was the attempt at communitarian experiments that sought to create new economic patterns for participants. Some of these experiments had a religious base, while others were essentially nonsectarian in character. The latter were best represented by the Fourierist associations, which advocated the creation of cooperative unions for communal living called "phalanxes." These were first proposed by the French socialist, Charles Fourier. In these units members were supposed to work at the tasks they found most congenial. In such an environment it was expected that a wholesome society would be achieved that would provide material equality. The ideas of Fourier were propagated in the United States by Arthur Brisbane, whose *Social Destiny of Man* analyzed "the vast and foolish waste which results from our present social mechanism and of the colossal economics and profits which would arise from Association and Combination in industrial interests."

Phalanxes were formed in several states, the most famous of which was Brook Farm, formed by New England Transcendentalists who banded together behind George Ripley to establish their phalanx in West Roxbury, Massachusetts, in 1841. Nathaniel Hawthorne and Orestes Brownson were two of the more illustrious "workers" at Brook Farm. Ralph Waldo Emerson and Bronson Alcott frequently visited—and lectured. Although the community never numbered more than 150 at most, it drew thousands of celebrity-watchers each year to gape at the members' extraordinary activity. Unfortunately, the experiment was not financially successful and was abandoned after a disastrous fire in 1847.

Another important communitarian experiment, but distinct from the Fourierist phalanx, was that founded by Robert Owen, the Scottish manufacturer known for his humanitarian reforms as an industrialist. He arrived in the United States in 1825 and founded his community, based on political and economic equality, in New Harmony, Indiana. Through collective ownership of property and co-operative labor, Owen expected to create a utopian society devoid of crime and poverty. "Who can even imagine," he wrote, "the change it will produce throughout society? The world has never yet seen a republic of cultivated freemen, but the next generation will see it. I would I might live to witness such a spectacle, afterwards, I could die contented and happy." Unfortunately, his advocacy of "free love" and atheism gave his experiment a bad name, and after a few years it failed. Even so, the basic idea inspired other men to attempt similar ventures in the ensuing years.

One such was the Oneida Community, founded in 1848 in Seneca Falls, New York, by John Humphrey Noyes, a divinity student. This community, numbering over 200 followers, emphasized manufacturing over agriculture and produced excellent silverware and steel products. It was one of the more enduring of the communitarian experiments despite some early difficulties over the founder's "free love" ideas and his efforts to produce superior children through the "scientific" mating of parents. Later, when its more unacceptable doctrines were purged, the Oneida community went on to achieve distinction for the quality of its manufactured products.

Of the religious communities—and there were many of these—perhaps the most unusual and intriguing was the Shaker movement, a split from English Quakers, founded by the charismatic Ann Lee Stanley (1736–84), or "Mother Ann Lee," who after a revelation that she should go to America, left Manchester, Great Britain and settled in Albany, New York, 1774. Deserted by her husband, she taught the sinfulness of sex and insisted on celibacy within the Shaker community. Like many other communitarians, she also preached the imminence of the millennium. In fact her "Believers" called themselves "The United Society of Believers in Christ's Second Appearance." Frugality, pacifism, and vegetarianism were other characteristics of this sect. Most curious of all was the ritual of singing and dancing practiced by the Believers. The violent shaking of the body, which gave the sect its unusual name, helped provide emotional release from the strictly disciplined lives they led.

After Mother Ann's death, leadership of the Shakers underwent a transition and followed a gender-neutral pattern of two co-leaders, one male and one female, reflecting Shaker belief in the duality of God, masculine and feminine, that God was both Mother and Father. While Christ was the masculine expression of

God's personality, Shakers held that Mother Ann was one of the feminine expressions. Although she died in 1784, the Shakers grew rapidly and by the Jacksonian era numbered over 8,000 converts living in nearly two dozen celibate communities from Maine to Florida. The curious who visited the communities—usually to see the dancing—were immediately struck by the beauty and simplicity of the surroundings. Buildings, furniture, farm tools, and leather goods were so masterfully crafted as to achieve an artistic distinction and inventiveness unrivaled by any other communitarian group. Indeed, the Shakers are generally credited with inventing the circular saw, the flat (as opposed to a round) broom, the washing machine, and the clothespin. Shakers also produced a great number of hymns, and although the sect is virtually extinct today, one of their hymns, "Lord of the Dance," is still popular among other religious groups, including Catholics.

But it was their unique form of dancing that intrigued the outside world. When they danced the Shakers wore thin dancing slippers and tiptoed into a large hall which was their meeting house to begin their dance. The singers, usually twelve to twenty in number, would take their places and then dancers would form the march, with men on the right and women on the left. They faced each other, standing approximately five feet apart and forming a circle. Frequently their hands would be raised, palms up, to symbolize the receiving of blessings. Then an elder would enjoin them to "go forth . . . and worship God with all their might in the dance." At that signal, the singers would commence their hymn, keeping time by swinging their arms and rising on their toes, and the dancers would then gallop around the room at top speed. Some of the sisters would whirl around like tops, eyes shut, for about fifteen minutes; others swayed to and fro, or pranced around in a circle and clapped their hands with such force that the sound resembled the report of pistols being fired into the air. They waved, clapped, swayed, whirled, and galloped until they verged on exhaustion. And not a word was spoken by any of them during the entire dance.

Another millennialist sect formed in the Jacksonian era was the Millerites. William Miller (1782–1849) who was born in Pittsfield,

Massachusetts and converted at a revival, studied the Bible on his own and predicted the Second Coming of Christ on October 22, 1844, at which time all true believers would ascend bodily into heaven. When the event failed to materialize, a more indefinite date was proclaimed. This sect has evolved into the Seventh-Day Adventist Church, a group known not only for its millennialist creed but its many works of charity and its widespread missionary efforts.

Another indigenous American religious movement was the Disciples of Christ, a society formed in 1809 by Thomas Campbell, a Presbyterian, who hoped to restore a primitive Christianity which had "neither creed nor name but only loyalty to Christ." His son, Alexander Campbell, shaped the society into a church and preached scriptural simplicity in organization and doctrine. In 1831 he united his congregation with Barton W. Stone's group of the Christian Church. The Christian Church resulted from the union of three evangelical groups, one Methodist, one Baptist and one Presbyterian, the latter led by Stone. This Christian/Disciples of Christ Church became the fastest growing denomination in America by the Civil War, numbering more than 100,000 members.

The religious zeal so characteristic of this Jacksonian age led many men and women to accept self-proclaimed "prophets" who claimed they could communicate with the supernatural, perform miracles, cure the sick, and raise the dead. One such "prophet," Robert Matthews, said he was not a Christian but a Hebrew, descended from the Israelites, and that his real name was Matthias. Rejecting Christianity as the work of devils, he announced that God the Father, in the person of Matthias, had returned to teach the truth and to gather the faithful to Zion. A journeyman carpenter who wore strange clothing, grew a beard and let his hair grow long—something quite unfashionable at the time—he seemed Christ-like to his those who heeded his call, but his fellow carpenters, in derision, dubbed him "Jumping Jesus." He founded the Kingdom of Matthias in Hudson, New York, promising only "real men" would be saved while everything bearing "the smell of women" would be destroyed. He controlled his followers through terror and prophecy, advanced bizarre religious doctrines, engaged in sexual irregularities and demanded absolute obedience from his followers. With money provided by his supporters he lived like a wealthy man. He impregnated the wife of one of his benefactors and claimed the child would become the Holy Son. Unfortunately the Holy Son turned out to be a girl. Described as part rogue, part fool, part lunatic, and part imposter, he was tried for murdering one of his followers but the evidence against him did not hold up in court, although he served thirty days in jail for contempt.

Matthews and others of his kind contributed substantially to one of the most extraordinary "sectarian inventions" that the United States, and indeed the world, has ever known. The dreadful events that occurred under Jim Jones in Guyana and David Koresh in Waco, Texas, during the latter part of the twentieth century when so-called prophets led their followers to their destruction, can be traced back to what happened in the Kingdom of Matthias.

Religious zeal gone mad also manifested itself by the rise of anti-Catholicism in which the Roman Catholic Church was described in gross and vulgar terms—"the whore of Babylon" was one—and priests and nuns were accused of sexual aberrations. The pope was portrayed as the antichrist in league with the devil. Worse, anti-Catholicism generated periodic violence. In 1834 an Ursuline convent in Charleston, Massachusetts, was burned by a frenzied mob, an action which prompted Catholics to threaten reprisals. The efforts to restrict the political power of Catholics continued to mount during the next two decades, culminating in the rise of the Know-Nothing party in the 1850s. No doubt part of the anti-Catholic crusade was a reaction to the influx of large numbers of Irish Catholics into the country following the famine in Ireland in the late 1840s. The number of Catholics in the country rocketed from 300,000 in 1830 to over 3 million thirty years later.

Unquestionably the most important religious innovation of the Jacksonian period was the appearance of a group which called itself the Church of Jesus Christ of Latter-Day Saints or, more popularly, the Mormon Church. Its founder, Joseph Smith (1805–44), was born in Vermont and raised in Palmyra, New York. He claimed to have supernatural visions when he was visited by the angel Moroni, who instructed him to unearth golden plates buried in a stone box which would provide an account of the lost tribes of Israel. Smith himself transcribed the plates from Old Egyptian. As published in 1830 the deciphered account constitutes *The Book of Mormon*, a name derived from a prophet who lived among the early settlers in America.

Smith gathered many followers to his new faith, especially from the lower economic classes who were attracted by his concern for the needs of the poor. He recorded the Prophet Nephi as saying of the elite: "They rob the poor because of their fine sanctuaries; they rob the poor because of their fine clothing; and they persecute the meek and the poor in heart because in their pride they are puffed up." He organized a religious oligarchy and a cooperative settlement. He led the faithful from New York to Ohio, then Missouri, and finally Nauvoo, Illinois, where a flourishing settlement of over 10,000 persons was founded. The hostility of neighboring towns, generated in part by the practice of polygamy by some of the leaders, led to Smith's murder in Carthage, Illinois. The Mormon community was seen by the outside world as a "brothel, sink of iniquity, Hades, and vortex of moral ruin."

After Smith's death, Brigham Young, a man brought up in desperate poverty and with little education, who responded to Smith's call, assumed control of the church. Under his aggressive and able leadership the Mormons abandoned Nauvoo in 1847 and moved across the plains into the Rocky Mountains, where they found a haven in the desert region alongside the Great Salt Lake. They established their church on a lasting basis, erected a cooperative commonwealth ruled as a theocracy, and soon had the desert blooming by means of irrigation obtained from the surrounding mountains. They called their settlement Deseret, meaning "honeybee." Despite many early difficulties the community survived and expanded. Thousands of Mormon converts journeyed across the continent to reach the settlement, many of them from Europe, where the Mormons carried their missionary appeal.

The Mormon church connected with the Jacksonian age because of its clear protest against the economic exploitation and oppression of the poor and its pride and belief in the central role of the American nation in God's plan. First off, the plates were found by Smith in New York. Moreover, the Book of Mormon explains God's interest in this country. And when Christ returns, according to the Mormon faith, He will come to the United States.

All told, the Jacksonian era was a remarkable and life-enhancing age. The reach for perfection by Americans, the attempt to adopt new patterns of life, join voluntary associations to eliminate crippling social disabilities, and to restructure their society underscored their vitality and "go ahead" mentality. Their preoccupation with money and material goods was offset to a considerable extent by their concern and regard for the less fortunate in society. Their moral values were rooted in their religious beliefs and their recognition of the worth of each individual. Their optimism was unbounded and infectious. They were a new breed. Their colonial and European past was gone. Their hope rested with the future.

CHAPTER SIX

The End of an Age

The Jacksonian age ended with a bang! The Mexican War ushered out an age of reform and advancing democracy and ushered in an age of sectional strife and eventual civil war. The old concerns about banks and tariffs and internal improvements dissolved in the scramble for empire and the implementation of a new ideology called Manifest Destiny.

Andrew Jackson had had a dream of empire from an early age, a dream that the United States would one day encompass "all Spanish North America." He advanced that dream by his seizure of Spanish-held Florida when sent by President Monroe to subdue the Seminole Indians along the southern border. That seizure enabled the President's Secretary of State, John Quincy Adams, to negotiate a treaty with Spain in which Florida was surrendered to the United States in consideration of $5 million worth of assumed claims by Americans against Spain, and the western boundary of the Louisiana Purchase was fixed at the Sabine, Red, and Arkansas Rivers and thence westward to the Pacific Ocean along the forty-second parallel. This treaty is sometimes called the Transcontinental Treaty because it gave the United States added claims to the Pacific Northwest, thereby stretching the nation from ocean to ocean. For Spain, the negotiations began as an attempt to save Texas and the territories behind it—which they succeeded in doing—and, if possible, to win a pledge from the United States not to recognize the independence of the South American colonies then in revolt, in return for which the indefensible Florida would be surrendered for a cash consideration. What resulted was the stimulation of American desire to become a transcontinental power.

Jackson had always encouraged that desire. Westward expansion, he contended, was essential to American security, especially in the area of the Southwest along the Gulf of Mexico. It was dangerous, he said, "to leave a foreign power in possession of heads of our leading branches of the great mississippi." Expansion was "necessary for the security of the great emporium of the west, Neworleans." Besides, "the god of the universe had intended this great valley to belong to one nation." And that nation—let no one doubt—was the United States.

Jackson's robust nationalism and fire-breathing expansionism explain his concern about the presence of the Spanish, the British, and the Indians on the continent and his driving determination to get rid of them. He had defeated all three militarily. As President he sought to expel them permanently from any position which would jeopardize American safety.

Like many southerners, Jackson believed that Texas had been acquired by the United States as part of the Louisiana Purchase. Adams had no right to relinquish it, he later declared. It is questionable whether Texas did in fact belong to the United States at the time the Transcontinental Treaty was signed, but southerners, apprehensive over northern reaction to the slavery issue during the Missouri debates and chagrined over limiting the spread of slavery beyond the 36°30' parallel within the Louisiana Purchase, argued that Texas belonged to the United States and should never have been surrendered. "How infatuated must have been our councils who gave up the rich country of Texas," Jackson wrote. And why had it happened? "It surely must have been with the view to keep the political ascendence in the North, and east, & cripple the rising greatness of the West." But he would attend to it, he told his friend John Coffee shortly after his inauguration as President. "I have long since been aware of the importance of Texas to the United States, and of the real necessity of extending our boundary west of the Sabine. . . . I shall keep my eye on this object & the first propitious moment make the attempt to regain the Territory as far south & west as the great Desert."

But he never got the chance. Mexico pulled itself free of Spanish rule and resisted every effort of the United States to purchase Texas. Several hundred American families immigrated to Mexico under an agreement worked out with Moses Austin and his son, Stephen F., in which sizable tracts of land were granted to the immigrants, along with home rule, on condition that the settlers acknowledged Mexican authority and became Mexican citizens. Thousands followed these first settlers, no doubt motivated by the economic depression resulting from the Panic of 1819. Many of them were slave owners from Tennessee, Alabama, and Mississippi who probably expected Texas to be annexed by the United States in short order. If so, their hopes were soon dashed. Jackson certainly wanted Texas, but he made an unfortunate appointment of a minister to treat with the Mexicans and nothing was gained except increased Mexican apprehension over American intentions.

The abolition of slavery in Mexico only heightened the demand of Texans for immediate annexation, and when Jackson failed to arrange a purchase of Texas they decided to take matters into their own hands. The Mexican authorities had already responded to the threat of dismemberment by attempting to centralize control over all parts of the Mexican Republic, thus diminishing Texan home rule. The distrust, apprehensions, and preparations for confrontation on both sides triggered open conflict in October 1835. The President of the Mexican Republic, General Antonio Lopez de Santa Anna, marched into Texas at the head of a 6,000-man army to reassert Mexican authority, and on March 2, 1836, Texas independence was proclaimed. One of Jackson's protégés, General Sam Houston, assumed command of the Texas army and at the Battle of San Jacinto on April 21, 1836, decisively defeated the Mexican army and captured Santa Anna. "We have barely room to congratulate every man who has Anglo-Saxon blood in his veins on the redemption of our brethren in Texas from Spanish power," declared the Washington *Globe*.

The Mexican minister to the United States, Manuel Eduardo de Gorostiza, angrily accused the United States of treachery and interference in the affairs of Texas. He emphasized his outrage by demanding his passports. Relations between the two countries seemed to be sliding toward war when, at a regular cabinet meeting, the Secretary of the Navy, Mahlon Dickerson, reported that he had received word from Commodore Alexander Dallas about "innumerable indignities" suffered by the American consul and residents at Tampico at the hands of Mexican authorities. Also, American armed vessels in the area had been refused water or permission for their officers to go ashore. Worse, the Mexican authorities threatened to put to death all Americans at Tampico in retaliation for the capture of Santa Anna.

Jackson flew into a rage. "Write immediately to Commodore Dallas," he barked at Dickerson, "& order him to blockade the harbour of Tampico, & to suffer nothing to enter till they allow him to land and obtain his supplies of water & communicate with the Consul, & if they touch the hair of the head of one of our citizens, tell him *to batter down & destroy their town & exterminate the inhabitants from the face of the earth!*"

The other members of the cabinet looked ashen. They were in a state of near shock. The President then turned to the Secretary of State and directed him to inform Gorostiza of the orders sent to Dallas. "Tell him, also," Jackson raged, "that we shall not permit … a citizen of the United States to be injured without taking immediate redress."

Fortunately, cooler heads prevailed and the citizens of Tampico were spared extermination. But relations between the United States and Mexico continued to deteriorate, with war a real and growing possibility. At one point the Texas Republic sent a commissioner, Samuel Carson, to Washington in the hope of winning U.S. recognition of Texas independence and eventual annexation. Jackson greeted him warmly at the White House. "Is it true, Mr. Carson," the President asked, "that your Government has sent Santa Anna back to Mexico?" Carson replied that Santa Anna was still in custody but would be freed momentarily in the hope that he could assist in winning Mexican ratification of the treaty recognizing Texas's independence.

"Then I tell you, Sir," said Jackson, "if ever he sets foot on Mexican ground, your Government may whistle; he, Sir, will give you trouble, if he escapes, which you dream not of."

Then, declared Carson, there would be war.

Jackson laughed. "Where is your means, Sir, to carry on an offensive war against Mexico?"

Carson brightened. "In the enthusiasms of the American people, their devotion to the cause of Liberty and the ways and means, to defray the expenses of the War," he cheerfully replied.

Before Jackson could respond to that remarkable statement they were interrupted by a summons to dinner and the conversation ended. But what neither Carson or Jackson knew was that General Sam Houston had decided not to release Santa Anna but to send him to Washington under guard to meet with Jackson in the expectation that the President could convince Santa Anna to let Texas go in peace.

A few weeks later the Mexican arrived in Washington looking relaxed and rested despite his long trip. Stolid, swarthy, with heavy features, a strong chin, and black hair plastered across his head, Santa Anna seemed the very personification of Mexican pride and bearing when he was introduced to President Jackson at the White House. "General Andrew Jackson greeted me warmly," Santa Anna recorded, "and honored me at a dinner attended by notables of all countries." Then they had a private talk. Jackson proposed that the United States extend its border to include Texas and northern California, in effect to run the line of the United States to the Rio Grande, up that river to the thirty-eighth parallel and then to the Pacific Ocean. As compensation, Mexico would receive $3.5 million. "But before we promise anything," Jackson continued, "Genl Santana must say that he will use his influence to suspend hostilities." What the United States wants most of all, the President added, "is to secure peace & tranquility on our respective borders & lay the foundation of a permanent tranquility between the U.S. and Mexico."

Santa Anna smiled. "To the Mexican Congress solely," he replied, "belongs the right to decide that question." So the interview ended on a polite but indefinite note. Not much later Jackson provided his guest with a warship to take him to Vera Cruz. But it was clear that the territorial craving of the United States now included not only Texas but California and the country north of it.

Given Jackson's expansionist dreams and his particular lust for Texas, it might be assumed that annexation would follow immediately. Indeed, many hoped that it would. But Jackson hesitated. He wavered and then drew back. Much as he hungered for Texas, he realized that immediate acquisition might ignite a war between the United States and Mexico. And what would the rest of the world think? They would surely see the acquisition as a brutal and aggressive act in violation of international law. When Stephen F. Austin appealed to Jackson for help, the President responded by saying that Austin "does not reflect that we have a treaty with Mexico, and our national faith is pledged to support it. The Texians [sic] before they took the step to declare themselves Independent, which has aroused and united all Mexico against them ought to have pondered well, it was a rash and premature act. Our nutrality [sic] must be faithfully maintained."

Milksop from Old Hickory! What a surprise! But probably he recoiled at the thought of the domestic strife certain to result from the acquisition of Texas, since the territory most assuredly would enter the Union as a slave state and thereby upset the balance between the rival sections of the country. He was especially concerned over what the abolitionists might do with this explosive issue. As a matter of fact he knew that they would exploit the opportunity to attack slavery throughout the nation by vigorously opposing admission. The Texas question, therefore, posed a real threat to the Union, one Jackson did not wish to risk.

There was another reason. His term in office would expire in another year and he was intent on winning the election of his hand-picked successor to the presidency, Martin Van Buren. Under no circumstances must the Whigs come to power. That would be disastrous. So Jackson backed away from a fight. His passion for the Union exceeded by far his passion for Texas. The best he could accomplish was recognition of the independence of Texas. What the United States and Mexico must do, he repeated many times, "is . . . lay the foundation of a permanent tranquility between the U.S. and Mexico." That in itself would be enough.

Van Buren did in fact succeed Jackson by winning election in 1836. But no sooner did he take office than the Panic of 1837 struck and virtually flattened his administration. Although it took several years to accomplish, he finally won an Independent Treasury System in 1840 to address the banking and money problems. Texas was left to its own devices and functioned as an independent republic from 1836 to 1845.

The hapless Van Buren was trounced by "Tippecanoe and Tyler, Too" in the log cabin campaign of 1840. This election outmatched the hijinks of the 1828 campaign in almost every respect. Complete with hard cider, rolling balls, coonskin hats, and other paraphernalia, the election reached extraordinary heights of hoopla and political nonsense. William Henry Harrison, the Whig candidate, was palmed off as another Andrew Jackson. He had won a modest (though usable) victory at Tippecanoe over the Shawnee Indians in 1811 and it provided superb propaganda in convincing the American people of his ability to lead the country out of depression and back to prosperity. "Van, Van, the used up man" was depicted as an effete easterner who had failed spectacularly as chief executive and had lost the confidence of the electorate.

Jackson was devastated. "The attempt by their mummeries to degrade the people to a level with the brute creation . . . by hard cider, Coons, Log cabins and big balls" will ultimately fail, he said. "The democracy of the United States have been shamefully beaten, *but I trust, not conquered."* Less than a month after his inauguration Harrison died of pneumonia, the first President to die in office. Jackson was ecstatic. "A kind and overruling providence has interfered to prolong our glorious Union and happy republican system which Genl. Harrison and his cabinet was preparing to destroy under the dictation of the profligate demagogue, Henry Clay."

The demise of the Whig President brought John Tyler to the presidential chair. A former Democrat who had deserted the party on account of Jackson's vigorous exercise of presidential power and handling of the Nullification Controversy, Tyler was a staunch advocate of Jeffersonian principles and could be expected to repulse any effort by the "profligate demagogue" to assert the principles and policies of the Whig party contradicted by his states rights philosophy.

Clay did attempt to engineer the repeal of the Independent Treasury and the creation of a new national bank and a higher tariff. But Tyler frustrated Clay's most cherished hope of another bank by killing the legislation with a veto. The Democrats loudly applauded. Said one: "Egad, Tyler has found one of old Jackson's pens and it wouldn't write any way but plain and straitforward." When a second bill was passed that tried to overcome the President's objections, Tyler again struck it down. And these vetoes split the Whig party from top to bottom. The entire cabinet, with one exception, resigned, and a body of Whig congressmen officially read Tyler out of the party. The single exception was the Secretary of State, Daniel Webster, who at the moment was completing negotiations for an important treaty with the British. He subsequently resigned but not until nearly a year after the conclusion of the negotiations.

In foreign affairs, the Tyler administration registered two notable achievements. The treaty Webster negotiated with Great Britain—the Webster-Ashburton Treaty (1842)—finally settled the northeast border between Maine and Canada. Approximately 12,000 square miles had been in dispute and the treaty divided the area almost evenly, with the United States receiving approximately 7,000 square miles. They also settled differences over the boundary area from Lake Superior to the Lake of the Woods, and the United States acquired the rich deposits of iron ore in the Mesabi Range in Minnesota, a fact neither side recognized at the time.

Tyler also acquired Texas. He named John C. Calhoun as his Secretary of State in 1844 and the two men committed themselves to acquiring the independent republic. What concerned them particularly was the effort of Great Britain to keep Texas independent under its own protection. Such an arrangement could bring the entire American west into jeopardy. England might attempt to unite Oregon with Texas and contend for California. It was also feared that it would persuade Texas to abolish slavery.

Although some Texans might wish to maintain their independence, many more followed the lead of Sam Houston and sought to bring about annexation by the United States. Texans not only felt a strong bond of kinship with their former country, but they needed the United States to protect them against the possibility of a renewal of war with Mexico.

On April 12, 1844, a treaty of annexation was signed by the representatives of the United States and Texas in which Texas would be admitted as a territory and surrender its public lands, in return for which the United States would assume Texas's debts up to a maximum of $10 million. It was understood that Texas would remain a slave-holding territory. The treaty was submitted to the Senate along with an accompanying letter from Calhoun to the British minister to Washington, Richard Pakenham. In it Calhoun declared that the treaty had been signed to protect American slavery from British attempts to bring about universal emancipation.

It was a foolish letter and it killed the treaty. Northern senators who favored annexation were outraged because "it would be death to them, politically, if they were to vote for the Treaty based on such principles." Meanwhile, the two national parties held their conventions and seemed prepared to nominate men who firmly opposed annexation. The Whigs eventually chose Henry Clay who, although a slave owner himself, feared that annexation would produce war with Mexico as well as excite sectional passions over slavery and prove financially prohibitive.

The Democrats had been expected to renominate Martin Van Buren but his opposition to annexation—he, too, feared the possibility of war and the likelihood of sectional hostility—set in motion a successful conspiracy to replace him. He was subsequently brushed aside in favor of the first dark horse in American history, James Knox Polk of Tennessee, known popularly as "Young Hickory." Polk was not actually unknown because he had served in the House of Representatives and had risen to the post of Speaker. He had also been elected governor of Tennessee. But most Democratic leaders did not think of him as a presidential possibility. In fact they rather regarded him as a excellent candidate for the post of Vice President, and Polk himself had agreed that that office was appropriate at this stage of his career. But he was a protégé of Old Hickory and an avid expansionist, and that made him particularly attractive to delegates from the South and Southwest. So, on the ninth ballot, he was unanimously nominated.

It proved to be a close race between Polk and Clay. The Democrats called for the reannexation of Texas and the reoccupation of Oregon, hoping by such territorial gains to win support from both the slave-holding South and the nonslave-holding North. By maintaining a balance the Union would be spared sectional conflict. At the last minute Clay attempted to equivocate on the question of the annexation of Texas but only succeeded in turning away antislavery votes in New York and Michigan. He said he would "be glad to see Texas admitted on fair terms," whatever that meant. "Slavery ought not to affect the question one way or another," he added.

But it did. And it defeated him. During the campaign the Democrats poked fun at his ambivalence.

> He wires in and wires out,
> And leaves the people still in doubt,
> Whether the snake that made the track
> Was going South, or coming back.

The popular margin of victory gave Polk 1.4 percent over Clay. It was a squeaker. "A mere *Tom Tit*," snorted John Quincy Adams, had bested "the old Eagle. The partial associations of Native Americans, Irish Catholics, abolition societies, liberty party, the Pope of

Rome, the Democracy of the sword, and dotage of a ruffian [Andrew Jackson] are sealing the fate of this nation, which nothing less than the interposition of Omnipotence can save."

Further American expansion now seemed inevitable. In fact, John L. O'Sullivan, editor of *The Democratic Review,* wrote an essay in 1845 in which he stated that American claim to the new territory in the west

. . . is by the right of our manifest destiny to overspread and to possess the whole of the continent which Providence has given us for the development of the great experiment of liberty and federative self government entrusted to us. It is a right such as that of the tree to the space of air and earth suitable for the full expansion of its principle and destiny of growth.

This theory of Manifest Destiny immediately captured the imagination of the American people as propagated by the many penny newspapers that had lately appeared. It expressed the sentiment and hope that Jackson had once put forward just prior to the War of 1812, namely, the acquisition by the United States of "all Spanish North America."

Capitalizing on this spirit and on Polk's victory, Tyler, in the closing days of his administration, declared that a majority of people advocated the annexation of Texas and he therefore proposed (and helped arrange) a joint resolution of both houses of Congress by which Texas would be admitted into the Union as a state and retain its public lands and debt. The resolution passed the Congress, and Tyler signed it on March 1, 1845. Texas ratified annexation on July 4 and was admitted into the Union as a slave state on December 29, 1845.

During the 1844 presidential campaign the Democrats had raised the cry, "Fifty-four Forty or Fight," meaning the "reoccupation" of all of Oregon up to the boundary of Russian Alaska at 54°40'. Actually Polk had designs on other territory and readily abandoned his extravagant claims in Oregon by agreeing to the forty-ninth parallel as the line separating Canada from the United States in the Northwest. A treaty was immediately worked out with Great Britain on June 15, 1846, which the Senate accepted, thus allowing the United

States to turn its attention to Mexico, where even bigger opportunities awaited the American expansionists.

What especially attracted Young Hickory was California, with its superb seaports fronting the Pacific Ocean and inviting expanded trade with the Orient. Thus, when the Mexican government again refused American efforts at purchase of this desired territory it became obvious that force would be necessary to educate Mexico about America's Manifest Destiny. Dispute over the southern boundary of Texas provided the excuse.

President Polk ordered General Zachary Taylor, whose troops were stationed on the Nueces River, to advance to the Rio Grande River, invading a kind of "no-man's land" between the United States and Mexico and virtually inviting Mexican attack. It came soon enough. On April 25, 1846, a detachment of Mexican troops crossed the Rio Grande, ambushed an American scouting party, and killed sixteen men. As soon as word of the ambush reached Washington, Polk notified Congress that Mexico had violated the border and "shed American blood upon American soil." Both houses immediately voted a declaration of war and on May 13, the President signed it.

The war brought total military victory to American arms. Even the capital of Mexico City was captured. Some of the more extreme expansionists in the United States actually considered absorbing the entire Mexican Republic. But the Treaty of Guadalupe Hidalgo, signed on February 2, and ratified in the Senate by a vote of 38 to 14 on March 10, 1848, proved less greedy. It not only ended the war but granted the United States title to 500,000 square miles of territory, including the present day states of California, Nevada, Utah, New Mexico, Arizona, a corner of Wyoming and the western slope of Colorado. It also recognized the Rio Grande as the border of Texas. In return the United States paid $15 million plus assumed claims of $3.25 million of its citizens against Mexico. American casualties in the war came to 1,721 from the fighting, and an additional 11,550 from disease. Both Henry Clay and Daniel Webster opposed the war and both lost sons in the conflict. Mexican casualties reached 50,000.

But the treaty also produced mounting resistance by abolitionists to the expansion of slavery into these new territories. Indeed, during the war itself, Representative David Wilmot of Pennsylvania offered an amendment on August 8, 1846, to an appropriation bill (the so-called Wilmot Proviso) that forbade the expansion of slavery into any territory to be acquired in the future, and the amendment won approval in the House but failed in the Senate.

It was ominous. Gone were the quarrels over the bank, the tariff, and internal improvements. Sectionalism and slavery replaced them. Southerners denied that Congress could prohibit the spread of slavery. Slaves constituted private property, they said, and property was protected under the Constitution. To outlaw slavery anywhere in the United States violated their rights and jeopardized liberty for all. Not only was their way of life under attack, they cried, but the very foundation of the American system of government as well. Their only recourse, if the demands of abolitionists triumphed, was separation. Secession. The end of the Union.

Andrew Jackson, who had died on June 8, 1845, just after the acquisition of Texas, had warned of the dangers of the slavery question. If the Union cracked, he said, it would take "oceans of blood & hundreds of millions of money" to repair. Within two decades of his death his prediction came true. A bloody civil war was necessary to bring about the final solution to the problem of slavery, which the statesmen of the Jacksonian Era could not resolve.

The broken-hearted Clay conjectured on what might have happened if he had been elected President in 1844 instead of Polk. "There would have been no annexation of Texas, no war with Mexico, no National debt . . . no imputation against us, by the united voice of all the nations of the earth, of a spirit of aggression and inordinate Territorial aggrandizement." The only thing Clay did not mention, for the simple reason that he was dead when it happened, was the real possibility that there might never have been a Civil War.

The slow, steady descent of the nation into raucous quarreling over sectionalism and slavery that resulted in the worst bloodletting in American history also ended an era—an era of reform, of advancing democracy, and of hope in what further glories the future would bring. Some Jacksonians actually warned that if the nation sank into the abyss of civil war over slavery, the "money power," the aristocracy, the elite would rise again out of the ruin and reestablish their oligarchic rule and make America once more the land of the rich and powerful. To some extent that is exactly what happened during the Gilded Age.

But the populistic spirit of the Jacksonian era, the reform impulse to improve society, and the passionate commitment to democracy did not end with the Civil War. Periodically they returned to steer the country away from greed and private interest to a compassionate concern for the welfare of all. Periodically the message of hope echoed across the land and galvanized the nation to renewed efforts to make the American dream a reality for all.

BIBLIOGRAPHICAL ESSAY

There is a vast literature on the Jacksonian age embracing all the myriad aspects of this dynamic and revolutionary period of American history. Fortunately a number of guides exist to aid a reader through this wilderness. I myself assisted Edwin A. Miles in compiling a list of all the books and articles relative to the period 1816–41 and published prior to 1979. They comprise nearly 5,000 titles and are grouped under various headings, both chronological and topical. The result was published by Harlan Davidson, Inc. of Wheeling, Illinois, as a volume in the "Goldentree Bibliographies in American History" series. Entitled *The Era of Good Feelings and the Age of Jackson, 1816–1841*, it is the most complete listing of published works on the Jacksonian period that I can recommend. For a bibliography on Jackson himself see Robert V. Remini and Robert O. Rupp, *Andrew Jackson: A Bibliography* (Westport, Ct., 1991) which is part of the Meckler Bibliographies of the Presidents of the United States series.

Alfred A. Cave, *Jacksonian Democracy and the Historians* (Gainesville, Fla., 1964) summarizes the important interpretations of the Jackson era written prior to its publication. Unfortunately, that was more than thirty years ago. Edward Pessen, in the newest edition of his *Jacksonian America: Society, Personality, and Politics* (Urbana, Ill., 1986), brings the historiographical discussion up to date in the lengthy bibliographical essay provided at the end of his book. Other useful interpretative guides include Edwin A. Miles's essay "The Jacksonian Era," which appeared in *Writing*

Southern History, edited by Arthur S. Link and Rembert W. Patrick (Baton Rouge, 1965); Charles G. Sellers, Jr., "Andrew Jackson versus the Historians," *Mississippi Valley Historical Review* 44 (1958): 615–634; and Ronald P. Formisano, "Toward a Reorientation of Jacksonian Politics: A Review of the Literature, 1959–1975," *Journal of American History* 63 (1976): 42–65. The bibliographical essay in Glyndon G. Van Deusen, *The Jacksonian Era, 1828–1848* (New York, 1959) includes instructive comments about the literature by the author.

There is perhaps no better way of entering the world of Jackson and his contemporaries than reading their own accounts of what was happening around them. Several of them left autobiographies, reminiscences, memoirs, histories, or sizable collections of papers and correspondence. For example, the *Correspondence of Andrew Jackson* (Washington, D.C., 1926–1935), edited in six volumes by John Spencer Bassett represents the best letters from a variety of collections of Jackson manuscripts. They include not only letters from Jackson but to him as well. The Jackson Papers Project, established originally at the Hermitage in Tennessee and recently moved to the University of Tennessee at Knoxville, has collected copies of every Jackson document extant, consisting in 1987 of approximately 60,000 items. These were microfilmed and issued in thirty-nine reels together with a *Guide and Index to the Microfilm Editions* (Wilmington, Del., 1987) prepared by Harold Moser, the director of the project. In addition, a letterpress edition of the most important documents is planned, four volumes of which have already been published and cover the period 1770–1820.

Many of the other leading personalities of this age also have comprehensive publication projects underway to make their papers available to the American public. These include John C. Calhoun, Henry Clay, Daniel Webster, and James K. Polk. As of 1996 the Clay and Webster projects have been completed: James F. Hopkins et al., eds., *The Papers of Henry Clay* (Lexington, Ky., 1959–92), 11 vols; Charles Wiltse et al., eds., *The Papers of Daniel Webster* (Hanover, N.H., 1974–89), 13 vols. And as of 1996, W. Edwin

Hamphill et al., eds., *The Papers of John C. Calhoun* (Columbia, S.C., 1959–), 22 vols, has arrived at 1846; while Herbert Weaver et al., eds., *The Correspondence of James K. Polk* (Nashville and Knoxville, Tenn., 1969–) has reached 1844. Of the major figures only Martin Van Buren lacks such a project, but his *Autobiography of Martin Van Buren*, AHA, *Annual Report for the Year 1918* (Washington, D.C., 1920) edited by John C. Fitzpatrick, is an important and extremely valuable source.

Other useful sources by a variety of participants in the events they narrate include Charles Francis Adams, ed., *Memoirs of John Quincy Adams*, 12 vols. (Philadelphia, 1874–77); Thomas Hart Benton, *Thirty Years View*, 2 vols. (New York, 1865); Reginald C. McGrane, ed., *The Correspondence of Nicholas Biddle* (Boston and New York, 1919); James A. Hamilton, *Reminiscences of James A. Hamilton* (New York, 1869); William Stickney, ed., *Autobiography of Amos Kendall* (Boston, 1872); and William J. Duane, *Narrative and Correspondence Concerning the Removal of the Deposits* (Philadelphia, 1838).

There are a number of contemporary witnesses to the Jacksonian age who were not always themselves directly involved in the dramatic events they record but who commented upon them or their society or provide background information that is invaluable. Some of the most noteworthy are: Allen Nevins, ed., *The Diary of Philip Hone, 1828–1851*, 2 vols. (New York, 1936); Gaillard Hunt, ed., *The First Forty Years of Washington Society* by Mrs. Samuel Harrison Smith, (New York, 1906); Henry S. Foote, *Casket of Reminiscences* (Washington, D.C., 1874); John W. Forney, *Anecdotes of Public Men* (New York, 1873); Benjamin F. Perry, *Reminiscences of Public Men*, 2 vols. (Philadelphia, 1883); Ben Perley Poore, *Perley's Reminiscences of Sixty Years in the National Metropolis* (Tecumseh, Mich., 1886); Nathan Sargent, *Public Men and Events*, 2 vols. (Philadelphia, 1875); and Henry A. Wise, *Seven Decades of the Union* (Philadelphia, 1881).

Nothing provides a more pleasurable and personal account of American society during the Jacksonian age than travel accounts by European visitors. And indeed some of them have written extremely perceptive analyses of men and events during the entire antebellum age. One of them, Alexis de Tocqueville, *Democracy in America*, 2 vols., (New York, 1945), is a classic work in American history and especially admired for its profound understanding and exposition of some of the most basic characteristics and ingredients of American life and institutions. There is no better place to start an investigation into Jacksonian society than this extraordinarily insightful book. An excellent critique of this work is James T. Schliefer, *The Making of Tocqueville's "Democracy in America,"* (Chapel Hill, N.C., 1980). See also A. S. Eisenstadt, ed., *Reconsidering Tocqueville's "Democracy in America,"* (New Brunswick, N.J., 1988).

There are other splendid accounts of American life by foreigners, even if they do not begin to compare with Tocqueville's imperishable work. Critical, indeed contemptuous at times but delightful nonetheless, is Frances Trollope, *Domestic Manners of the Americans* (London, 1832). And the following can also be read with considerable profit: Harriet Martineau, Society in America (London, 1837), and *Retrospect of Western Travel*, 2 vols. (New York, 1838); Michel Chevalier, *Society, Manners and Politics in the United States* (Boston, 1839); Francis J. Grund, *Aristocracy in America*, 2 vols. (London, 1839); Captain Frederick Marryat, *A Diary in America* (London, 1839); Thomas Hamilton, *Men and Manners in America* (Philadelphia, 1833); J. S. Buckingham, *America* (London, 1841); Captain Basil Hall, *Travels in North America in the Years 1827–1828* (Philadelphia, 1829); and Frances A. Kemble, *Journal*, 2 vols. (London, 1835).

Because so many of the leading figures of the Jacksonian era were larger than life and statesmen of the first rank there have been any number of outstanding monographs written about them, both biographies and specialized studies of individual events or movements. Jackson himself has been particularly fortunate—at least in terms of the writing quality of the many biographies written about him over the last hundred and more years. But then he led such an exciting and eventful life that it is difficult to speak about him without catching some of the vigor and energy that he always seemed to exude. Apart from the campaign biographies and narratives written by his friends—of which the John Reed/ John H. Eaton study (Philadelphia, 1817) and the life by Amos Kendall (New York, 1844) still merit attention—the first attempt at a serious, indeed scholarly, analysis of Old Hickory's life was executed by James Parton, the so-called father of American biography. His three-volume *Life of Andrew Jackson* (New York, 1859, 1860) remains an important source and statement about Jackson's life and career. Parton traveled extensively to gather material for his study and without his research we would know relatively little about Jackson's early life. As to his overall interpretation, Parton came away with rather ambivalent feelings about Old Hickory and his democracy. At times in the work Parton sneers at the mindless mob "who could be wheedled, and flattered, and drilled," but at other times he lauds the democratic advances achieved under Jackson and declared them the mark of an enlightened society. What caused Parton the most difficulty was the "spoils system." This he could not abide. It was an abomination in his sight. Rotation, he "consider[ed] an evil so great and so difficult to remedy, that if all his other public acts had been perfectly wise and right, this single feature of his administration would suffice to render it deplorable rather than admirable." No matter. For many good reasons Parton's work remains a major statement about Jackson, even though it is over a hundred years old. In the first place Parton researched his subject rather thoroughly, considering what was available to him, and managed to interview or get written statements from a number of principal figures of the period who were still alive, including Sam Houston, William B. Lewis, Francis P. Blair, and several others. Secondly, he is a very reliable historian who was extremely careful about his facts and is consistently accurate in what he reports. Furthermore, the *Life* is written with enthusiasm and panache. All the characters are three-dimensional and come sweeping off the pages in life-like detail. So graceful and artless was the writing that some early critics dismissed the work as journalistic.

Jackson's next biographer, William Graham Sumner, the early sociologist, published his *Andrew Jackson* in 1882. It was the seventeenth volume in the American Statesmen Series, edited by John

T. Morse, Jr., and was critical of its subject from start to finish, deploring in particular Jackson's flawed moral character and emotional excesses. But Sumner is less interested in Jackson per se than in his administration and, in particular, such economic questions as the Bank, the tariff, and internal improvements. The author's commitment to laissez-faire economics and Social Darwinism found expression in this biography, for Old Hickory provided a superb vehicle for the propagation of these fashionable ideas. Other early historians, such as Herman von Holst and James Schouler, joined Sumner in his criticism of the Jacksonian era and constituted what one student has called a "liberal patrician" or "Whig" school of history. Most of these critics came from European middle- or upper-middle-class families. They were well educated, and a few of them had seen public service. Because their class had been ousted from political power by the arrival of a mass electorate, these historians were biased against Jacksonian Democracy, and their books reflect their Whiggish prejudice.

The restoration of Old Hickory and his friends to respectability among historians probably began with the appearance in 1893 of the vastly influential article by Frederick Jackson Turner, "The Significance of the Frontier in American History," reprinted in numerous anthologies. Turner argued that American democracy fundamentally emerged from the wilderness. Naturally Jackson and his followers were seen as the very personification of this frontier democracy, who carried it eastward with them when they came to power. The thesis was approved, amplified, and propagated by such distinguished historians as Charles A. Beard, Vernon L. Parrington, and a number of others of the early twentieth century who were caught up in the reform movement of the Progressive era. They regarded the Jacksonian era as an "Age of Egalitarianism" that produced "The Rise of the Common Man." Jackson himself was applauded as a "Man of the People." Thus the Progressive school of historiography completely overwhelmed and replaced the Whig or "liberal patrician" school.

This interpretation dovetailed rather well with the general views of Alexis de Tocqueville. During his visit, Tocqueville discovered a widespread belief in egalitarianism and cited it as one of the distinctive traits in the American character. His democratic liberalism—augmented by the works of the Progressive historians, especially Turner, Beard, and Parrington—dominated historical thought about the American past for the next fifty years or more. Massive buttressing of the argument was especially provided by the economic interpretation of Charles Beard. Even today there are a number of historians who are still basically influenced by the Tocqueville-Turner-Beard approach to history. One major biography of Jackson reflecting the thinking of the Progressive school appeared in 1910. This was John Spencer Bassett's *The Life of Andrew Jackson*, 2 vols. (New York, 1916), a sound and scholarly study—indeed the author was the first professionally trained scholar of Jackson and his era—written almost entirely from documentary material by Jackson and his friends.

In virtually all of the works of these Progressive historians the importance of geographic sections in the nation was stressed. Class difference did not play a central role in their thinking and, indeed, on one occasion, Turner denied any class influence in the formation of frontier democracy. The only important historian to naysay Jackson or his democracy during this period was Thomas P. Abernethy, whose *From Frontier to Plantation in Tennessee: A Study in Frontier Democracy* (Chapel Hill, 1932) declared Old Hickory not only a frontier aristocrat, but an opportunist and a land speculator who strongly opposed the democratic forces in his own state of Tennessee.

Then, in 1933 and 1937, Marquis James published his superbly written two-volume biography of Jackson, *The Border Captain and Portrait of a President* (Indianapolis and New York), which was later reissued as one volume, *The Life of Andrew Jackson* (1938). The work won the Pulitzer Prize but it simply treats Jackson as democratic champion and hero, nothing more.

The inevitable termination of the dominance of the Progressive school's interpretation of Jacksonian Democracy came with the publication in 1946 of certainly the most important historical monograph written about this era: *The Age of Jackson* (New York, 1945) by Arthur M. Schlesinger, Jr. It is a landmark study and represents the beginning of modern scholarship on Jackson and his era.

Simply presented, Schlesinger argued that class distinctions rather than sectional differences best explain the phenomena of Jacksonian Democracy. He interpreted the actions of the Jacksonians as an effort of the less fortunate in American society to combat the power and influence of the business community. Workers in the cities, he insisted, constituted the most solid core of support for the Jacksonian movement. The ideology of Jacksonianism evolved from the conflict between classes and best expressed its goals and purposes in the problems and needs facing urban laborers. Schlesinger chose the Bank War to highlight the conflict, and it made an excellent choice for his purposes. To understand what Jacksonian Democracy is all about, he said in effect, a student must first understand the Bank War. What attracted many historians to this pathbreaking study was the fact that Schlesinger provided a clearer definition of Jacksonianism and a more precise explanation of its origins than had been available before.

Schlesinger's work was immediately hailed as a major contribution to the study of American history, and it received numerous and well-deserved prizes and awards. But there were critics as well, and they appeared almost immediately. Bray Hammond, in a series of articles as well as in his *Banks and Politics in America from the Revolution to the Civil War* (Princeton, 1957), and Richard Hofstadter in his *The American Political Tradition and the Men Who Made It* (New York, 1948), contended that the Jacksonians were not the champions of urban workers or small farmers but, rather, ambitious and ruthless entrepreneurs principally concerned with advancing their own economic and political advantage. They were "men on the make" and frequently captains of great wealth. According to Hofstadter, the Jacksonians were not so much hostile to business as they were hostile to being excluded from business by the old-money elite. Where Schlesinger had emphasized conflict in explaining the Jacksonian era, Hofstadter and those who agreed with him insisted that consensus best characterized the period. This entrepreneurial thesis, as it was called, found strong support from many young scholars who constituted the Columbia University school of historians. In a series of articles and books produced by these critics, they managed to reduce the Old Hero to little more than an opportunist, a strike breaker, a shady land speculator, and (for some) a political fraud.

Marvin Meyers in his *The Jackson Persuasion*, (Stanford, Calif., 1957), added a fascinating twist to the entrepreneurial thesis by arguing that Jacksonians did indeed keep their eyes focused on the main chance, like the sharp-eyed, sharp-nosed businessmen they were, but at the same time they yearned for the virtues of a past agrarian republic. They hungered after the rewards of commerce but looked back reverentially on the blessings of a less hectic and simpler agrarian society.

Another sharp redirection of Jacksonian scholarship developed shortly after the publication of Lee Benson's *The Concept of Jacksonian Democracy: New York as a Test Case* (Princeton, 1961). This work suggested a whole new approach to the investigation of the Jacksonian age by employing the techniques of quantification to uncover historical facts. Moreover, Benson placed his emphasis on social questions and found that such things as ethnicity and religion played a far more important role than economics in determining how a person voted or which party won his allegiance. He regarded the Jacksonian rhetoric about democracy and the rights of the people as "claptrap" and insisted that local issues in elections meant much more to the voters than national issues.

The ethnocultural school of historical writing that developed following the publication of Benson's study rejected class difference as an important factor in political determinism. Proponents of this school asserted that German and Irish Catholics, for example, were more likely to vote Democratic because of their ethnicity and religion than any other factor. Besides, some argued, the wealth among Whigs was not materially greater than the wealth among Democrats. Edward Pessen, in his *Jacksonian America: Society, Personality, and Politics* (Homewood, Ill., 1969) and *Riches, Class and Power Before the Civil War* (Lexington, Mass., 1973), among a number of other books and articles, went one step further and asserted that Jacksonian America was not particularly egalitarian in terms of wealth, as Tocqueville had observed. He rejected the argument that the common man came into his own politically during the Jacksonian age and declared that the country was still run by the uncommon men of the day, the economic elite. By the end of the 1970s the ethnocultural approach had been displaced somewhat by cultural Marxists, who reemphasized class conflict in analyzing voter preference. Other historians eschewed this approach and worked to describe or portray what might be called a "political culture" for the period. Nevertheless, many of the insights provided by the ethnocultural school still find their way into the studies of other historians who are not strictly quantifiers themselves. For example, such historians as Joel Silbey, Sean Wilentz, and Harry L. Watson contend that the electorate normally develops a wide set of values based on many factors, including class, religion, nationality, family, residence, employment, and age, and then invariably votes to safeguard those values as they perceive them. See Harry L. Watson, *Jacksonian Politics and Community Conflict: The Emergence of the Second American Party System in Cumberland County, North Carolina* (Baton Rouge, 1981); Sean Wilentz, *Chants Democratic: New York City and the Rise of the American Working Class, 1788–1850* (Princeton, 1984); and Joel Silbey, *Shrine of Party: Congressional Voting Behavior, 1841–1852* (Pittsburgh, 1967) and *Political Ideology and Voting Behavior in the Age of Jackson* (Englewood Cliffs, N.J., 1973).

Watson particularly has demonstrated by his study of North Carolina politics that national issues did in fact matter in general elections. Even Jackson has been somewhat restored to his former importance, if not his former heroic stature. See Douglas R. Egerton, "An Update on Jacksonian Historiography: The Biographies" *Tennessee Historical Quarterly* 46 (1987): 79–85. Robert V. Remini's three-volume life of Old Hickory: *Andrew Jackson and the Course of American Empire, 1767–1821; Andrew Jackson and the Course of American Freedom, 1822–1832; Andrew Jackson and the Course of American Democracy, 1833–1845* (New York, 1977, 1981, 1984) reemphasizes Schlesinger's findings and Jackson's faith and commitment to liberty and democracy. He contends that Jackson was in fact a man of the people, just as the Progressive historians had argued, and that he actively attempted to advance democracy by insisting that all branches of government, including the courts, reflect the popular will. A one-volume condensation of the three volumes has since been made available and is entitled *The Life of Andrew Jackson* (New York, 1988). Remini's views were further expanded in his *The Legacy of Andrew Jackson: Essays on Democracy, Indian Removal and Slavery* (Baton Rouge, 1988). He also revealed for the first time the fact that Jackson became the vassal of the King of Spain in 1789 in an article, "Andrew Jackson Takes an Oath of Allegiance to Spain," in the *Tennessee Historical Quarterly* 54 (1995): 2–15.

A relatively recent and most stimulating and provocative new interpretation of the first half of the nineteenth century is provided by Robert H. Wiebe in his *The Opening of American Society: From the Adoption of the Constitution to the Eve of Disunion* (New York, 1984). In this work Wiebe sees an "unplanned accumulation of activities" (such as the emergence of popular politics and the rise of economic self-determination) during the Jacksonian era which provided Americans in most instances with the freedom to choose, and they seized this power of choice whenever they spotted it and guarded it zealously once they had it. Out of it developed a democratic society that virtually annihilated everything erected by the revolutionary gentry except "the shell of their Constitution," but it also enhanced the development of a truly national state.

Besides Jackson, most of the principal figures of this era have received excellent biographical treatment. Two recent studies of Van Buren's life are particularly fine: John Niven, *Martin Van Buren and the Romantic Age of American Politics* (New York, 1983), and Donald B. Cole, *Martin Van Buren and the American Political System* (Princeton, 1984). These biographies should be supplemented by Major L. Wilson, *The Presidency of Martin Van Buren* (Lawrence, Kan., 1984). John C. Calhoun has also been well served by several biographers: Charles M. Wiltse, *John C. Calhoun*, 3 vols. (Indianapolis and New York, 1944–1951), Margaret L. Coit, *John C. Calhoun, American Portrait* (Boston, 1950); John Niven, *John C. Calhoun and the Price of Union: A Biography* (Baton Rouge, 1992) and Irving H. Bartlett, *John C.*

Calhoun (New York, 1993). A superb study of Daniel Webster is Maurice C. Baxter, *One and Inseparable: Daniel Webster and the Union* (Cambridge, Mass., 1984). See also Irving Bartlett, *Daniel Webster* (New York, 1978); Sydney Nathans, *Daniel Webster and Jacksonian Democracy* (Baltimore, 1973); and Norman Brown, *Daniel Webster and the Politics of Availability* (Athens, Ga., 1968); and Richard Current, *Daniel Webster and the Rise of National Conservatism* (Boston, 1955). The most recent full-scale biography of Henry Clay is Robert V. Remini, *Henry Clay: Statesman for the Union* (New York, 1991). Calvin Colton, *The Life and Times of Henry Clay*, 2 vols. (New York, 1846) though old is still useful, as is Glyndon G. Van Deusen, *The Life of Henry Clay* (Boston, 1937). A splendid treatment of arguably the three greatest Senators in American history is Merrill D. Peterson, *The Great Triumvirate: Webster, Clay, and Calhoun* (New York, 1987). See also George R. Poage, *Henry Clay and the Whig Party* (Chapel Hill, 1936); Carl Schurz, *Life of Henry Clay*, 2 vols. (Boston, 1937); Clement Eaton, *Henry Clay and the Art of American Politics* (Boston, 1957); and Maurice G. Baxter, *Henry Clay and the American System* (Lexington, Ky., 1995). Other outstanding biographies include William N. Chambers, *Old Bullion Benton, Senator from the New West* (Boston, 1956); Samuel F. Bemis, *John Quincy Adams and the Foundations of American Foreign Policy* and *John Quincy Adams and the Union*, 2 vols. (New York, 1949, 1956); the unfinished biography of James Knox Polk by Charles G. Sellers, Jr., *James K. Polk, Jacksonian, 1795–1843* (Princeton, 1957), and *James K. Polk, Continentalist, 1843–1846* (Princeton, 1966); John Munroe, *Louis McLane, Federalist and Jacksonian* (New Brunswick, N.J., 1973); Thomas P. Govan, *Nicholas Biddle, Nationalist and Public Banker* (Chicago, 1959); Elbert Smith, *Francis Preston Blair* (New York, 1980); and Robert Seager II, *And Tyler Too: A Biography of John and Julia Gardiner Tyler* (New York, 1963). The biography of John Quincy Adams by Samuel F. Bemis should be supplemented by Mary W. M. Hargreaves, *The Presidency of John Quincy Adams* (Lawrence, Kan., 1985), and the unfinished biography of James Knox Polk by Charles G. Sellers, Jr., should be supplemented by Charles A. McCoy, *Polk and the Presidency* (Austin, Tex., 1960), and Paul H. Bergeron, *The Presidency of James K. Polk* (Lawrence, Kan., 1987).

The best overview of politics in the Jacksonian era is Harry L. Watson, *Liberty and Power: The Politics of Jacksonian America* (New York, 1990). Robert V. Remini, *Martin Van Buren and the Making of the Democratic Party* (New York, 1959) analyzes Van Buren's central role in Jackson's election in 1828. Some of the political changes are traced in detail in Richard P. McCormick, *The Second American Party System: Party Formation in the Jacksonian Era* (Chapel Hill, 1966); Richard Hofstadter, *The Idea of a Party System* (Berkeley, 1969); Shaw Livemore, *The Twilight of Federalism: The Disintegration of the Federalist Party, 1815–1830* (Princeton, 1962); and Ronald P. Formisano, *The Birth of Mass Political Parties: Michigan, 1827–1861* (Princeton, 1971). How Jackson's image was superbly used for political advantage by contemporaries is described in John William Ward, *Andrew Jackson, Symbol of an Age* (New York, 1955). Another stimulating work which contrasts the goals and purposes of the Whigs and Democrats is Major L. Wilson, *Space, Time, and Freedom: The Quest for Nationality and the Irrepressible Conflict* (Westport, Conn., 1974). And the best study of the shenanigans introduced by parties to stimulate voter interest in presidential elections is Robert G. Gunderson, *The Log Cabin Campaign* (Lexington, Ky., 1957). For the 1828 election, see Robert V. Remini, *The Election of Andrew Jackson* (New York, 1963); and for the 1832 election see Samuel Rhea Gammon, *The Presidential Campaign of 1832* (Baltimore, 1922). Two contrasting interpretations of Jackson's presidency can be found in Donald Cole, *The Presidency of Andrew Jackson* (Lawrence, Ka., 1993), Richard B. Latner, *The Presidency of Andrew Jackson: White House Politics, 1829–1837* (New York, 1937) is especially good.

Intellectual historians have contributed a great deal to our understanding of this age by explaining the concept of "republicanism" and its impact on the leading figures of antebellum America. An excellent introduction is Robert E. Shalhope, "Toward a Republican Synthesis: The Emergence of an Understanding of Republicanism in American Historiography," and "Republicanism and Early American Historiography," *William and Mary Quarterly* 29 (1972), 49–80, 39 (1982), 334–356. For a different view of the question see Joyce Appleby, *Capitalism and a New Social Order* (New York, 1984).

The rise of the Whig party is carefully detailed by E. Malcolm Carroll, *Origins of the Whig Party* (Durham, N.C., 1925). The ideology of the party is traced in Daniel Walker Howe, *The Political Culture of the American Whigs* (Chicago, 1979), and Daniel Walker Howe, ed., *The American Whigs: An Anthology* (New York, 1973). See also Thomas Brown, *Politics and Statesmanship: Essays on the American Whig Party* (New York, 1985); Arthur C. Cole, *The Whig Party in the South* (Washington, 1913); Paul Murray, *The Whig Party in Georgia, 1825–1853* (Chapel Hill, 1948); and Henry H. Simms, *The Rise of the Whigs in Virginia, 1824–1840* (Richmond, 1929). For the Anti-Masons, the most recent study is Paul Goodman, *Towards A Christian Republic: Antimasonry and the Great Transition in New England, 1826–1836* (New York, 1988). Also helpful is William P. Vaughn, *The Anti-Masonic Party in the United States, 1826–1843* (Lexington, Ky., 1983).

On the development of American democracy, in addition to Tocqueville, there are several worthwhile monographs, among which are: Chilton Williamson, *American Suffrage from Property to Democracy, 1760–1860* (Princeton, 1960); Louis Hartz, *The Liberal Tradition in America* (New York, 1955); Moisie Ostrogorski, *Democracy and the Organization of Parties*, 2 vols. (New York, 1902); Patrick T. Conley, *Democracy in Decline* (New York, 1977); George M. Dennison, *The Dorr War: Republicanism on Trial, 1831–1861* (Lexington, Mass., 1976); and Marvin E. Gettleman, *The Dorr Rebellion: A Study in American Radicalism* (New York, 1973).

For the Bank War a useful survey is Robert V. Remini, *Andrew Jackson and the Bank War* (New York, 1967), but it can be supplemented with a number of valuable studies: John M. McFaul, *The Politics of Jacksonian Finance* (Ithaca, 1972); William G. Shade,

Banks or No Banks: The Money Question in Western Politics, 1832–1865 (Detroit, 1972); Peter Temin, *The Jacksonian Economy* (New York, 1969); James R. Sharp, *The Jacksonians Versus the Banks: Politics in the States after the Panic of 1837* (New York, 1970); William Gouge, *A Short History of Paper Money and Banking in the United States* (New York, 1968); Ralph C. H. Catterall, *The Second Bank of the United States* (Chicago, 1903); Sister M. Grace Madeleine, *Monetary and Banking Theories of Jacksonian Democracy* (New York, 1970); and Fritz Redlich, *The Moulding of American Banking* (New York, 1968). On the panic of 1837 see Reginald C. McGrane, *The Panic of 1837* (Chicago, 1924).

The Indian problem is most capably described in Ronald N. Satz, *American Indian Policy in the Jacksonian Era* (Lincoln, Neb., 1975). But the definitive study of Indian policy throughout American history is Francis Paul Prucha, *The Great Father: The United States Government and the American Indians*, 2 vols. (Lincoln, Neb., 1984). See also his *American Indian Policy in the Formative Years* (Lincoln, Neb., 1962), and "Andrew Jackson's Indian Policy: A Reassessment," in *Journal of American History*, LVI (1969), 527–539. A most controversial but fascinating study is Michael Paul Rogin, *Fathers & Children: Andrew Jackson and the Subjugation of the American Indian* (New York, 1975). On removal itself, see Arthur H. DeRosier, Jr., *The Removal of the Choctaw Indians* (Knoxville, 1970); Grant Foreman, *Indian Removal: The Emigration of the Five Civilized Tribes* (Norman, Okla., 1953); Anne H. Abel, *The History of Events Resulting in Indian Consolidation West of the Mississippi* (Washington, D.C., 1908); and Wilson Lumpkin, *The Removal of the Cherokee Indians from Georgia*, 2 vols. (New York, 1907). John K. Mahon, *History of the Second Seminole War, 1815–1842* (Gainesville, Fla., 1967); Cecil Eby, *"That Disgraceful Affair": The Black Hawk War* (New York, 1973), and Ellen M. Whitney, comp. and ed., *The Black Hawk War, 1831–1832*, 2 vols. (Springfield, Ill., 1970, 1975) describe the two important Indian wars of the Jacksonian period.

The best and most recent treatment of nullification is Richard E. Ellis, *The Union at Risk: Jacksonian Democracy, States' Rights and the Nullification Crisis* (New York, 1987). Of particular value is Kenneth M. Stampp, *The Imperiled Union: Essays on the Background of the Civil War* (New York, 1980). Also useful are Merrill D. Peterson, *Olive Branch and Sword—the Compromise of 1833* (Baton Rouge, 1982); William W. Freehling, *Prelude to Civil War: The Nullification Movement in South Carolina, 1816–1836* (New York, 1966); and Frederic Bancroft, *Calhoun and the South Carolina Nullification Movement* (Baltimore, 1928). On slavery and sectionalism, see: William J. Cooper, Jr., *The South and the Politics of Slavery, 1828–1856* (Baton Rouge, 1978); Drew Faust, ed., *The Ideology of Slavery: Pro-Slavery Thought—the Antebellum South, 1820–1860* (Baton Rouge, 1980); Paul Finkelman, *An Imperfect Union: Slavery, Federalism and Comity* (Chapel Hill, 1981); Robert W. Fogel and Stanley L. Engerman, *Time on the Cross: The Economics of American Negro Slavery*, 2 vols. (Boston, 1974); Alison Goodyear Freehling, *Drift Toward Dissolution: The Virginia Slavery Debate of 1831–1832* (Baton Rouge, 1982); James Oakes, *The Ruling Race: A History of American Slaveholders* (New York, 1982); Stephen B. Oates, *The Fires of Jubilee: Nat Turner's Fierce Rebellion* (New York, 1974); David Potter, *The South and the Sectional Conflict* (Baton Rouge, 1968); Robert S. Starobin, ed., *Denmark Vesey: The Slave Conspiracy of 1822* (Englewood Cliffs, N.J., 1970); Charles Sydnor, The Development of Southern Sectionalism, 1819–1848 (Baton Rouge, 1948); J. Mills Thornton, *Politics and Power in a Slave Society* (Baton Rouge, 1978); and Richard C. Wade, *Slavery in the Cities* (New York, 1964).

The best overview of slavery is Peter Kolchin, *American Slavery, 1619–1877* (New York, 1993). Kenneth Stampp, *The Peculiar Institution* (New York, 1955) is also valuable. So too Eugene Genovese, *Roll, Jordan, Roll: The World the Slaves Made* (New York, 1974), and the classic study by John Hope Franklin, *From Slavery to Freedom: A History of American Negroes* (New York, 1980).

For abolitionism, the best modern study is James Brewer Stewart, *Holy Warriors: The Abolitionists and American Slavery* (New York, 1976). An excellent account of the intellectual background of the abolitionist movement is *Lewis Perry, Radical Abolitionism: Anarchy and the Government of God in Anti-Slavery Thought* (Ithaca, 1973). Useful but older is Louis Filler, *The Crusade Against Slavery* (New York, 1960). On racism, see Leon F. Litwack, *North of Slavery: The Negro in the Free States, 1790–1860* (Chicago, 1961) and Ira Berlin, *Slaves Without Masters: The Free Negro in the Antebellum South* (New York, 1974).

On such questions as economic change, tariffs, internal improvements, public lands, and related topics, the following are valuable: Thomas C. Cochran, *Frontiers of Change: Early Industrialism in America* (New York 1981), Charles Sellers, *The Market Revolution* (New York, 1993), Douglass C. North, *The Economic Growth of the United States* (Englewood Cliffs, N.J., 1961), Stuart Bruchey, *The Roots of American Enonomic Growth, 1607–1861* (New York, 1965), Malcolm J. Rohrbough, *The Land Office Business* (New York, 1968), Daniel Feller, *The Public Lands in Jacksonian Politics* (Madison, Wis., 1984); Carter Goodrich, *Government Promotion of American Canals and Railroads, 1800–1890* (New York, 1960); Benjamin H. Hibbard, *A History of the Public Land Policies* (Madison, Wis., 1965); Philip D. Jordan, *The National Road* (Indianapolis, 1948); Edward Stanwood, *American Tariff Controversies in the Nineteenth Century*, 2 vols. (Boston, 1928); Frank W. Taussig, *The Tariff History of the United States* (New York, 1888); George Rogers Taylor, *The Transportation Revolution, 1815–1860* (New York, 1951); and Gavin Wright, *The Political Economy of the Cotton South: Households, Markets and Wealth in the Nineteenth Century* (New York, 1978).

A study of the courts and legal processes that is particularly good for the Jackson years is Morton Horwitz, *The Transformation of American Law, 1780–1860* (Cambridge, Mass., 1977). Also valuable are Kermit L. Hall, *The Politics of Justice: Federal Judicial Selection and the Second Party System, 1829–1861* (Lincoln, Neb., 1979); Carl B. Swisher, *Roger B. Taney* (New York, 1935); and Charles Warren, *The Supreme Court in United States History*, 2 vols. (Boston, 1922). For administrative history and the spoils system see Leonard D. White, *The Jacksonians: A Study in Administrative History, 1829–1861* (New York, 1954); and Sidney

H. Aronson, *Status and Kinship in the Higher Civil Service: Standards of Selection in the Administrations of John Adams, Thomas Jefferson, and Andrew Jackson* (Cambridge, Mass., 1964).

Until recently not much scholarly work had been done on Jackson's foreign policy, but that void has been happily filled by John M. Belohlavek, *"Let the Eagle Soar!": The Foreign Policy of Andrew Jackson* (Lincoln, Neb., 1985). Other works treating aspects of foreign affairs for the entire era include: David M. Pletcher, *The Diplomacy of Annexation: Texas, Oregon, and the Mexican War* (Bloomington, Ind., 1973); William C. Binkley, *The Texas Revolution* (Baton Rouge, 1952); Justin H. Smith, *The Annexation of Texas* (New York, 1911); Frederick Merk, *Slavery and the Annexation of Texas* (New York, 1972); Norman A. Graebner, *Empire on the Pacific: A Study in American Continental Expansion* (New York, 1955); K. Jack Bauer, *The Mexican-American War, 1846–1848* (New York, 1974); Justin H. Smith, *The War with Mexico* (New York, 1919); and Otis A. Singletary, *The Mexican War* (New York, 1960). On westward expansion, see Frederick Merk, *History of Westward Expansion* (Cambridge, Mass., 1978); Ray Allen Billington, *The Far Western Frontier, 1830–1860* (New York, 1956) and *Westward Expansion: History of the American Frontier* (New York, 1974). On Manifest Destiny see Albert K. Winberg, *Manifest Destiny* (Baltimore, 1935); and Frederick Merk, *Manifest Destiny and Mission in American History* (New York, 1963). A controversial examination of the subject is Thomas R. Hietala's *Manifest Design: Anxious Aggrandizement in Late Jacksonian America* (Ithaca, 1985). For an excellent account of the Mexican War's impact on American society, see Robert W. Johannsen, *To the Halls of Montezuma* (New York, 1985).

A fairly comprehensive survey of the reform movements of the Jacksonian era is Alice Felt Tyler, *Freedom's Ferment* (Minneapolis, 1944), but a more recent overview is Ronald G. Walters, *American Reformers, 1815–1860* (New York, 1978). An excellent anthology of writing by reformers is Walter Hugins, ed., *The Reform Impulse, 1825–1850* (New York, 1972). For the connection between religion and reform, see William G. McLoughlin, *Reviv-*

als, Awakenings, and Reform (New York, 1978) and his *Modern Revivalism: Charles Grandison Finney to Billy Graham* (New York, 1959); Timothy L. Smith, *Revivalism and Social Reform in Mid-Nineteenth Century America* (New York, 1957); Charles C. Cole, Jr., *The Social Ideas of the Northern Evangelists, 1826–1860* (New York, 1954); Cifford S. Grifford, *Their Brother's Keeper: Moral Stewardship in the United States, 1800–1865* (New Brunswick, N.J., 1960); Dickson D. Bruce, *And they All Sang Hallelujah: Plain-Folk Camp-Meeting Religion, 1800–1845* (Knoxville, 1974); Charles A. Johnson, *The Frontier Camp Meeting: Religion's Harvest Time* (Dallas, 1955); and William W. Sweet, *Revivalism in America* (New York, 1949). See, especially, Whitney R. Cross, *The Burned-Over District: The Social and Intellectual History of Enthusiastic Religion in Western New York, 1800–1850* (Ithaca, 1950). A frightening new look into the excesses of religious fervor in this period can be found in Paul E. Johnson and Sean Wilentz, *The Kingdom of Mathias: A History* (New York, 1994). On Mormonism, an excellent work is Jan Shipps, *Mormonism: The Story of a New Religious Tradition* (Urbana, Ill.,1985).

For Transcendentalism consult Paul F. Boller, Jr., *American Transcendentalism, 1830–1860: An Intellectual Inquiry* (New York 1974); Van Wyck Brooks, *The Flowering of New England* (Boston, 1936); Merle E. Curti, *The Growth of American Thought* (New York, 1943); Donald Koster, *Transcendentalism in America* (Boston, 1975); Rush Welter, *The Mind of America, 1820–1860* (New York, 1975); and Francis O. Matthiessen, *American Renaissance; Art and Expression in the Age of Emerson and Whitman* (New York, 1941).

Of particular reforms for the Jacksonian era the reading selection is especially rich. Some of the best works include David Rothman, *The Discovery of the Asylum* (Boston, 1971); William J. Rorabaugh, *The Alcoholic Republic* (New York, 1979); Lawrence A. Cremin, *American Education: The National Experience* (New York, 1980); Carl Bode, *The American Lyceum* (New York, 1956); Barbara J. Berg, *The Remembered Gate: Origins of American Feminism* (New York, 1977); Nancy Cott, *The Bonds of Woman-*

hood (New York, 1977); Barbara Welter, *Dimity Convinctions: The American Woman in the Nineteenth Century* (Athens, Oh., 1976); Leonard L. Richards, *"Gentlemen of Property and Standing": Anti-Abolition Mobs in Jacksonian America* (New York, 1970); and Michael Feldberg, *The Turbulent Era: Riot and Disorder in Jacksonian America* (New York, 1980).

Among many studies of Jacksonian society, see especially Rowland Berthoff, *An Unsettled People: Social Order and Disorder in American History* (New York, 1971); Russel B. Nye, *Society and Culture in America* (New York, 1970); Douglas T. Miller, *Jacksonian Aristocracy* (New York, 1967); *Stow Persons, The Decline of American Gentility* (New York, 1973); Thomas Bender, *Community and Social Change in America* (New York, 1978); Sam B. Warner, Jr., *The Urban Wilderness: A History of the American City* (New York, 1972). On southerners, see Wilbur J. Cash, *The Mind of the South* (New York, 1941); Frank L. Owsley, *Plain Folk of the Old South* (Baton Rouge, 1949); and Bertram Wyatt-Brown, *Southern Honor: Ethics and Behavior in the Old South* (New York, 1983).

INDEX

The Jacksonian Era, Second Edition
Copy editor and production editor: Lucy Herz
Proofreader and photo editor: Claudia Siler
Printer: Thomson-Shore, Inc.